ANGEL VISITS
FROM BIPLANE TO JET

Frank Griffiths

ANGEL VISITS

FROM BIPLANE TO JET

FRANK GRIFFITHS

Thomas Harmsworth Publishing
London

By the same author:
Winged Hours

ACKNOWLEDGEMENTS

I wish to thank the Proprietors of Blackwoods Magazine for
permission to reprint the substance of two articles 'The
Ways of a Walrus' and 'French Gravity'; also Group
Captain Harley Boxall for permission to use his verbatim
report which gave such a graphic description of his existence
as a castaway on uninhabited Ko Rawi Island.
Finally my thanks to Douglas Fisher of Douglas Fisher Audio
Visual Ltd of Mistley for permission to use his photographs
and for his companionship on so many of my winged hours.

F.G.

ISBN O 948807 02 4

Printed in Great Britain by
The Bath Press, Avon

FOREWORD

When Frank Griffiths – 'Griff' as we all knew him – asked me to write a Foreword to his second book, I felt sure that his story would be in a humorous vein and packed with light-hearted anecdotes; in this I was not disappointed.

This absorbing book describes a number of widely varying activities in which the author took part, spanning his long career as an RAF pilot from the pre-war days until his retirement in the 1960s. He recalls vividly his part in the move of a Blenheim squadron from England to Singapore in 1939 – a most demanding and hazardous flight, particularly with non-existent navigational aids and the monsoon weather to contend with.

Griffiths' account of the research work in developing airborne radar – research which had such a far-reaching impact on the prosecution of the air war – makes fascinating reading, and throws new light on the pioneer work carried out in the early years. He describes the painstaking scientific effort that went into the development of an automatic landing system, and it is interesting to reflect how long it all took before such a system was introduced into regular airline use.

In this book Frank Griffiths has given us a series of stories which graphically illustrate some of the outstanding achievements of the 'Back-Room Boys and Girls' – people who were never in the limelight but whose contribution to victory was incalculable. His own personality and sense of fun come out fully in these accounts, and his ability to see the humorous side of life has not changed in the forty years of our friendship.

Air Chief Marshal Sir Lewis Hodges,
KCB, CBE, DSO, DFC.

INTRODUCTION

'Would you prefer a seat in the Smoking or Non-smoking section, Sir?' enquired the exquisitely groomed mammalion at the check-in desk.

I am a nervous passenger in aircraft. I would have liked to have replied 'An aisle seat please, near an emergency exit and over the black box'. An aisle seat because I suffer from claustrophobia in any other seat. Over the black box because it is so placed in the aircraft that it will receive least damage in an incident. Designers know what they are doing, for aircraft rarely fly backwards into a mountain; so they place the black box in the tail. But it is also that part of the aircraft which experiences the most movement, and the tail can be uncomfortable.

Knowing that the aircraft would be a 747 I elected for Row 40 which has plenty of leg room and is alongside the galley and an emergency exit.

I was bound for New Zealand from London by British Airways and our first sector of eight hours from Heathrow passed mainly in slumber as we mushed through the night to a dawn landing at Bombay.

By the time we had refuelled in Bombay the air temperature had risen considerably. I was only too well aware that the warmer the air temperature, the more runway we would need to become airborne. The next sector,

Bombay to Perth, was a long one, and with a full load of passengers, thirty-two thousand gallons of fuel aboard, and an all-up weight of 350 tons, we should need all the runway the Indians could allow us.

As a passenger I always look at the second hand of my watch immediately the power comes on for take off. It is a curious fact that while different aircraft take off at different speeds they all seem to take the same amount of time to leave the ground – forty seconds.

But in very hot conditions, or at high-altitude airfields, you cannot blame the aircraft for wanting to stay on the ground a little longer.

There is a moment on the take off run known as the 'abort time', when you can still cut the power if you want to, and stop the aircraft before you run out of concrete. After the abort time you must go on, and it says much for modern aviation that today's aircraft, even if they lose one engine, can still get airborne on the remaining power available.

On this very warm February morning I had reckoned our abort time at about 26 seconds.

We started our take off run. At 18 seconds there was a loud bang. From my seat in Row 40 I could see a pack of black playing cards pouring out of the after-end of the No 1 (outer port) engine as it got rid of its turbine blades on to the runway.

Immediately I was thrown forward into my lap strap, as the reverse thrust, brakes and spoilers took effect. We stopped just before going into the Indian Ocean.

The cabin crew drill was impeccable. They probably didn't feel the deceleration, because they sit *in backward-facing seats;* but they had their hands on the handles of the emergency doors and remained in this tensed condition until at least a minute after we had stopped.

For twenty minutes we remained stationary while things cooled down, then under our own power we taxied to a remote part of the airfield, and with everybody fully relaxed, we ate our curry lunch aboard the aircraft before being dispersed to hotels.

I learned later that we had probably ingested some rubbish into No 1 engine. Because the outer engines on the big jets hang down near the ground during the take-off run they have a vacuum cleaner effect. It was only an incident; and due to crew discipline a small one. But it took me back to the days when we were researching passenger safety. That research, which we did immediately after the War, strongly suggested that backward-facing seats were much safer. This was because in the event of sudden deceleration passengers were in an automatic crash position, their heads and bodies being fully supported.

During my years of active flying, six of which were at research establishments concerned with radar, automatic landings and air safety in its many different forms, I experienced several incidents far more serious than this one. But such flying is not the only subject of my tale. The story starts at the beginning of the War in the Far East.

The title of the book is taken from words of Thomas Campbell, as was that of my previous book, *Winged Hours*. 'What though my winged hours of bliss have been, like angel-visits...' The choice is deliberate. It is designed to imbue the two tales with a sense of unity.

Frank Griffiths

CHAPTER 1

Ferry to the Far East

It was a strange scene. Black night, a star studded sky and, looking down from the walls of the ancient fort, the sinister shadows of Blenheim aircraft silhouetted on the desert by the floodlights on the battlements.

An hour before dawn, still sultry with heat to a European; but the galabieh-clad guards, clutching their ancient rifles, crouched against the walls of the fort as though to draw warmth from them.

It was the fourth hour of the First of September 1939 at Sharjah in the Persian Gulf.

Briefing was in the dining room. Very informal. 'You'll have a headwind to Karachi but if the monsoon doesn't blow too hard you should make it in about four hours. There shouldn't be any cloud. Not over the sea anyway'.

Only four hours! In our short nosed Blenheims we only carried fuel for four and a half hours. Oh well! We would just have to make sure that we didn't get lost!

This was Day Nine of the move of No 62 Squadron RAF from Cranfield in Bedfordshire to Singapore. If we did make Karachi we should have flown, as a complete squadron, five thousand miles in seven flying days. There had been rumours of war when we left England and each day we expected to receive a signal telling us to turn back. But no signal came. Perhaps there wouldn't be war after all. Chamberlain had

1

said so last year hadn't he? 'Peace in our time', he said as he waved his piece of paper and we 'stood by', our aircraft dispersed round the airfield at Cranfield. We couldn't have dropped any bombs then for the Blenheim was a comparatively new introduction to the Air Force. We hadn't any bomb racks. Still we could have taken some good photographs!

Now it was different. We were a highly trained unit and we had the bomb racks but we were going in the wrong direction!

What a wonderful feeling it was to be in the desert during those few moments before the dawn; but we had no time to contemplate. With baggage aboard, I climbed last into my Blenheim and the desert silence was shattered by 24 Mercury engines bursting into life. In the time it took to warm engines the night turned to full daylight and the sun's orb was on the horizon. We took off in threes as usual and headed East climbing rapidly. Rapidly, not only to clear the mountains of the Western Hajar but to keep the aircraft cool.

Oh the thrill of flying over the desert at dawn with two great Mercury engines pulling you heavenwards! The feeling of elation is the same as riding to hounds or skiing. It somehow seemed immoral that I was being paid to enjoy such a feeling. While we flew in formations of three aircraft, we all navigated independently knowing that there would be times when bad weather or engine failure would mean breaking formation. With no proper navigating position Sergeant Willmott sat beside me using his thumb, a small protractor, a ruler and a driftsight. Leading Aircraftsman Pidd, the fitter, lay curled up on the engine covers between the mainspars like a dog in a basket. Right aft, crouched in his gun turret, Aircraftsman Templeton fiddled with a most ancient transmitter/receiver, its bottle valves glowing faintly. He was to prove, in the end, our sole external navigational aid. Yet what lowly ranks these prewar experts enjoyed!

Unlike Malta, India was big enough to find. At least we

shouldn't miss it. Not that the flight from Marseilles to Malta had posed any problems. It was trying to find Mersa Matruh after leaving Malta that had upset my ego. We set a direct course across the Mediterranean with nothing to see en route except sea. On arrival at the coast of North Africa the question had arisen as to whether to turn left or right for there was nothing to see except sand. My leader, Ken Powell, turned right and we followed. Luckily I had been asked to take a last minute passenger in Malta. A French Naval Officer of very high rank who wished to join his ship in Alexandria as soon as possible. Being so senior I had asked him to occupy the seat next to me and banished Willmott to share the doghole with Pidd from which position he 'navigated' peering over the Naval Officer's shoulder.

We flew west for twenty minutes after we struck the coast and then came to an indentation. 'C'est Sidi Barani là bas' said the NO. 'Vous êtes trop à l'oeust'. He seemed a very experienced officer with a rugged lined face and like so many naval officers had crows feet at the outer corner of his eyes. His appearance gave me confidence.

For want of any better aids (Templeton wasn't doing too well with his transmitter at this time) we turned East and after 30 minutes flying we arrived at Mersa Matruh! I felt subdued. We hadn't had a problem like this at my navigation school. This boob taught me a lesson. If you want to find somewhere on a coastline after a long sea crossing make a deliberate error by heading to one side of the destination, then, when you make your landfall, at least you know which way to turn.'

So this time we were to head for a point 20 miles south of Karachi and we'd then turn left when we reached India, as Pakistan was then known.

We could see the coast of Iran and then Baluchistan away on our left. It was comforting to know that the map seemed to be fairly accurate; and then the coast disappeared for two hours. Rather anxious hours but eventually land appeared ahead . . . India.

I was looking forward to seeing elephants, palaces, green jungle and the mighty Indus but when we reached the coast it was just desert! Maybe I hadn't read the right books. The Province of Sind was just as much a desert as Oman, and the Indus, when we came to it, a mere trickle.

So we arrived at Drigh Road, Karachi and there again was another mooring mast for the R 101. We had already flown from one mast at Cardington then another mast at Abu Sueir, Egypt. What sad memorials these masts were to the airship era which never materialised.

While the aircrews enjoyed five days rest at Karachi, Pidd and his fellow fitters worked all hours servicing the Blenheims for the other half of the journey. I was intrigued to see parked in one of the hangars the biggest four engined biplane in the World at that time. This was the Imperial Airways 'Scylla'. She was in mothballs but was to fly again and do sterling work in the Far East in the coming conflict.

Although four days had elapsed since war was declared and we had been expecting a recall signal to the UK each day, no signal came. Surely they couldn't fight the war without 62 Squadron? So there was nothing for it but to obey our present orders and press on towards Singapore.

Next came the desert leg to Jodhpur; a superb lunch arranged by the Maharajah and on to Allahabad with the monsoon clouds getting lower and more menacing every minute. We flew in very loose formation as usual and as the clouds came down the hills grew higher. Then my starboard engine lost power and started backfiring.

The Blenheim I had plenty of power and although it was then impossible to feather a propeller, it was possible to maintain height on one engine with the other propeller wind-milling in coarse pitch. We flew on dropping further and further behind the formation until we were alone. Willmott quickly worked out a course to the nearest airfield which was

Jhansi. In due course we arrived to find the landing ground completely covered by water with only a windsock to show its approximate position. The monsoon had certainly reached Jhansi.

There was nothing for it but to fly on to Allahabad where we arrived well after everyone else. The engine was ruined as a piston had disintegrated.

Allahabad was a revelation. It was like stepping back to the days of the mutiny. Although I had now been three years in the Royal Air Force I had not yet been in an Army Officers Mess. Here we were accommodated in the Officers Mess of the 1st Battalion the Queen's Royal Regiment and it was to give me a look into the life of the pukka sahib before it was to disappear for ever. At every meal a servant stood behind each officer's chair. The display of silver on the dining room table was beyond description. Remarking on the magnificence and quantity of the silver to an officer he replied 'Yes, it is rather fine but this is merely a remnant. All our best stuff was lost when the *Birkenhead* went down in 1852'! Yet despite this magnificence we enjoyed earth closets and baths in a tin tub filled by bearers with discarded four-gallon petrol cans!

I had to stay for seven days while we obtained a new engine from Umbala. We did the engine change by borrowing an ammunition hoist tripod from the fort which they said had been on the inventory since the mutiny. A quick air test nearly ended in disaster when I stupidly landed downwind through not having noticed the wind change caused by a line squall.

On the 16th September we roared off at dawn with lowering angry monsoon clouds building up. A quick refuel at Calcutta and on to Rangoon, only to return to Calcutta an hour later very frightened and humble after our first battle with the monsoon. With our modern powerful Blenheims and superb blind flying instruments we thought we were omnipotent. 'You shouldn't fly in the afternoon – no one

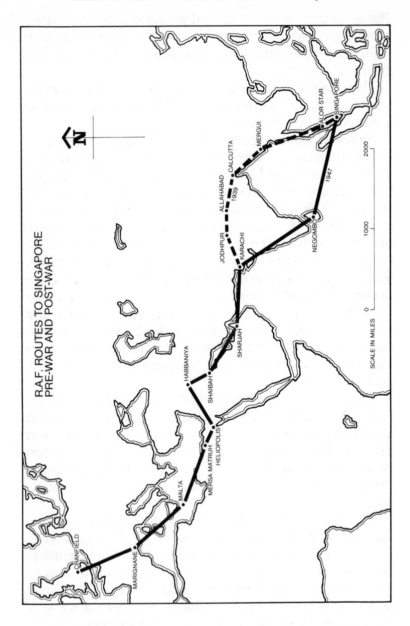

6

does' was all the sympathy we received from the control tower at Calcutta!

We had learnt a lesson; so next morning we started off really early to try and beat the monsoon build-up. We made Rangoon in four hours, a quick refuel and then a two hour trip to a curious red laterite strip cut out of the rubber trees at Mergui.

As I taxied back along the laterite strip to the landing end a curious sight came into view. To the side of the runway was a small parking area and here sat 'Jupp of Mergui', Lord of all he surveyed, on the back of a bullock. Over his head was held a huge umbrella to protect him from the sun! I was not able to determine his exact position in our empirical hierarchy. Jupp was reputed to be ex Royal Navy and a cockney who had been in Burma since 1911 when 'he missed his ship'. The story may not have been true but he was known as 'The Ruler of Mergui' and certainly behaved and looked like a Far Eastern Potentate of the time of Marco Polo. His hospitality was much appreciated but we had little time for socialising. All hands had to get down to refuelling. A ghastly business throwing endless four gallon cans of fuel up onto the wing having first knocked two holes in the can with an axe. On the wing Pidd and Templeton would pour the fuel into huge funnels in each of which was a washleather. It was most impressive the way fuel would rush through the washleather but any water was held back; and there was plenty of water for the fuel had been in stock a long time. Our remaining airborne depended on the efficiency of the washleathers. They were guarded like jewels and never never used for cleaning purposes.

A quick cold beer for each man and off to Alor Star in Malaya in the hope that we might beat the sun and find the afternoon monsoon less active the further south we flew.

We left in the usual formations of three aircraft and were soon in trouble and had to break formation and climb for dear life. Huge cumulo-nimbus clouds were down to ground level and these gave us no other alternative but to climb and fly through them. We hadn't any oxygen so I levelled off at 14,000 feet. The turbulence was so bad that it was merely a question of 'keeping the little aeroplane on the artificial horizon' of the instrument panel. A reasonably safe process when you didn't know whether you were going up or down or turning or whether it was Christmas or Easter. There are moments in aeroplanes when you just have to trust in something and appear calm and collected so that the crew don't detect that you are in a blind funk. This was one of them.

I noticed the vertical speed indicator winding itself up at 3000 feet per minute despite the fact that I was, apparently, straight and level and it must have been right because the altimeter was showing 18,000 feet and now driving snow was coming into the cockpit through the illfitting windows. We shivered in our shorts and open necked shirts then suddenly we were 'dropped' to 14,000 feet while still straight and level! Rulers, pencils, maps and various bits and pieces glued themselves to the roof of the aircraft. Glancing back to check the morale of the crew I saw that Pidd had been levitated on to the ceiling of the fuselage sitting on a magic carpet of engine covers.

With no position check as to our whereabouts we set course for Alor Star when, by our watches, we thought we had reached the end of the Victoria Peninsula. We had to be careful not to fly over Siam now that war had broken out. Siam was neutral.

Over the sea the intense turbulence eased, but not my anxiety for I had no idea how we were to break cloud to find Alor Star. It was somewhere in this area where Kingsford Smith* had recently disappeared. From the map the sea was strewn with islands, some of considerable height. To an

---

* Kingsford Smith disappeared in this area on a flight UK to Australia in the 1930's.

aeroplane there is nothing harder than a cloud full of mountain.

At last, Templeton, who was working the Direction Finding station at Alor Star on 333 kcs, a frequency beloved of W/T operators, received a first class bearing. A quick plot by Willmott confirmed that on this bearing it was safe to let down and we finally broke cloud in intense rain at 800 feet over the sea. At times we passed the odd island and one at least was shaped like a tomato sauce bottle and almost reached the cloud. I couldn't help but think; had Kingsford Smith hit one of these?

We flew on using first class bearings obtained by Templeton, a quick flash of mangrove swamp, orderly rubber plantations, bungalows with shining tin roofs and an airfield. Oh joy of joys, it was Alor Star.

We all made it except for Ken Powell who had had the misfortune to be given reciprocal bearings. He had therefore flown away from Alor Star instead of towards it! Presumably the civilian chinese ground operator was too busy and harassed to check his sensor for direction. Just before dark a last faint message came through from Powell 'Force landing now' then silence and fading hopes.

By dawn however we knew that Powell and his crew were safe. He had pulled off a spectacular landing on a road in Siam. It was not his fault that he had been lost. He and his crew were interned however because Siam was neutral. A month later Powell and his crew and his Blenheim arrived on a train at Singapore, and the aircraft was little the worse for being dismantled.

The next day came the last stage to Tengah, a new airfield some 14 miles from Singapore City on the Western half of the island. A short two hour flight in good weather and we arrived as a squadron in close formation. Only one aircraft was missing. Had there not been a war in progress to steal the news our flight might have made headlines for it was the first really long distance flight of a land based squadron. This achievement was the outcome of two years of intensive training. It is sad to recall that from this time onwards the squadron achieved little, except the award of one VC.

The war was far from Singapore yet flying had to be curtailed to preserve aircraft for the conflict which was bound to come some day. Pilots were only to fly for three hours each month. It was difficult to keep everyone busy and morale suffered. Fortunately our Station Commander was a Group Captain Oliver Bryson MC, DFC and bar, AM (Albert Medal) and he kept us busy; in the mornings at any rate and for some of us most of the night as well.

He had a fine physique but was a capacious drinker. Wary officers would escape by any avenue rather than be caught by him in the anteroom during the evening; if they were they knew that they wouldn't get away till morning! It is true that the morning started very early under Oliver Bryson's regime; 5 am would see the officers in PT kit starting through the rubber trees on a 'run-walk-run' which might extend to four miles.

Oliver Bryson was trained as a cavalry officer in 1914, transferred to the Royal Flying Corps and had been attached with a flight of Bristol Fighters to the White Russian Army. His stories were endless and interesting if you could manage to stay awake through the night. Oliver himself never slept at night but only in the afternoon 'rest period'.

He allowed us to play cards in the offices to pass the time but only Bridge was allowed. It improved the mind he said and to be caught playing 'vingt et un' meant running two laps round the airfield and an extra orderly officer duty! He had all the commissioned ranks down at the scrap dump from time to time salvaging every nut and bolt we could find.

Each of us, in a fit of patriotism surreptitiously applied for repatriation to the UK so that we could take part in the war. Oliver called us together and said 'I've had these applications placed in front of me and I am tearing them all up. I've already had one war and believe me before this lot is over you'll be sick of war so you'll all stay where you are'. He was right.

Poor Oliver. He eventually 'did for himself' in a big way. One evening he had been on the town and bought a tiger skin complete with head. Just before midnight he made a convivial entry into the Tanglin Club on all fours clad only in the tiger skin and his underpants. Furthermore the underpants didn't quite cover him (this was in the days before 'Y' fronts were invented). He roared his way across the dance floor. We junior officers loved him for it!

Unfortunately very high ranking civil and military personages and their ladies were present and Oliver left for England by sea two days later. We were sorry to see him go. In spite of his idiosyncrasies he was a great leader.

The amenities of Tengah itself increased sensationally when, early in 1940, we moved into the new Officers' Mess, reputed to be 'the most beautiful and luxurious building east of the Taj Mahal!' My room had a verandah and a superlative view, and each officer had his own bathroom. As a crowning felicity, in a continent where, east of Iraq, I had not found a single WC with a chain which pulled, in the new Mess there was 52 lavatories, all with infallible chains, for 38 officers.

But my chief delight was in the fine opportunities for sailing at Tengah. There was so little work to do that the RAF were encouraged to take leave, and I spent most of my leave afloat. I bought a native boat, a koleh, very fast and very easy to capsize; and later a yacht named *Marionella* in which I cruised whenever I could, chiefly with Ken Hutchins ('Hutch') and 'Pongo' Scarf. Two days before Christmas 1939 we sailed up the Malacca Straits. On Christmas Eve we called on some Malay lighthouse keepers at Pulo Pisang Island and were most hospitably received. Christmas morning saw us sailing up the main street of Kukup, an island village on stilts, to do our shopping. Later in the day, when we were out of sight of land, we rescued two exhausted Malays whose sailing koleh had capsized, a common enough experience which they usually dealt with easily, but in this case there was too much sea running. We bailed them out and sent them on their way. We ate our Christmas dinner by moonlight anchored off a coral reef at Raffles Island.

Chapter 2

Pulo Rawi

Our life at Tengah was boring in the extreme. Oliver Bryson did his best to keep us occupied with his dawn runs through the rubber plantations, retrieving nuts and bolts from the scrap dump, swinging compasses, sessions on the range firing rifles and revolvers etc but we weren't exactly thrilled by these activities. One interesting task however, we did have, and that was detachment duty up at Alor Star.

This detachment's task was to fly daily over to the Dutch Harbour of Sabang at the northern tip of Sumatra where six German merchantmen were waiting to make a break out. Holland was neutral at this time and the ships had every right to take shelter in a neutral harbour. The daily reconnaissance was required to see if they were still there and what were the latest colours they were painted. Over the horizon *HMS Danae* waited.

On 4th April 1940 I was on duty in the Ops Room at Tengah when Flying Officer Harley Boxall and his crew left Alor Star on this routine mission.

We were aroused out of our usual torpor with a message that a W/T call had been received from the aircraft saying that they had lost a propeller in the air on their way back from Sabang and that they were landing at an island called Pulo Perak. This was the cause of great concern for Pulo Perak rose straight out of the sea and was an impossible place to land.

13

Losing a propeller was to become a common fault with overseas Blenheims. In this case it was probably due to seizing through lack of oil which in turn was caused by heavy oil consumption through operation off desert strips without efficient air intake filters. When the engine seized the heavy metal propeller would decide to fly on its own. Very disconcerting to the pilot and crew.

Within twenty minutes we had a flying boat from 230 Squadron circling Pulo Perak for it happened to be in the vicinity at the time but it saw no trace of Harley Boxall's Blenheim or the crew which they had rather expected to find in a rubber dinghy on the water.

The search was continued daily until it was certain that the aircraft must have sunk in the sea without trace. The crew were reported to their families as 'Missing – Believed Killed'.

However Harley and his crew survived and here is his story in his own vivid words:

'I levelled off at 6,000 feet and sat relaxed at the controls as we flew at a steady 170 knots homeward bound – mission accomplished.

Two and a half hours earlier we had taken off in our Blenheim from Alor Star in Malaya on a photographic reconnaissance of German shipping in the harbour of Sabang, at the northern tip of Sumatra in the Dutch East Indies. Holland had not yet been drawn into the War.

We had 300 miles to go across the Straits of Malacca when the oil pressure of the starboard engine began to fluctuate and the engine showed signs of overheating. I throttled back, but within minutes the oil pressure dropped to zero and a dreadful shuddering shook the aircraft as the engine seized. The propeller twisted itself off its shaft, dropped into space and disappeared into the ocean beneath.

I increased power on the port engine to maintain altitude. Because we had valuable photographs and vital information to deliver, I decided to press on and attempt the 300 mile sea crossing on one engine; the unacceptable alternative was to fly back the odd 50 miles and make a forced landing in Sumatra but this inevitably would have meant internment for, as far as one could see at the time, the duration of the War.

After about half an hour the port engine, labouring under the increased revolutions, began to overheat. I reduced power to the minimum and our airspeed dropped to 90 knots. This was not much above stalling speed and the aircraft felt very soggy as I endeavoured to keep her on course. The trimming tabs fully extended would not keep her straight and I had to exert constant pressure on the rudder bar; I could only keep her level by holding up the starboard wing with full aileron control. We limped along like this for over an hour, when an island appeared through the thick haze beneath. Just at this moment the oil pressure of the port engine became erratic and, within seconds, this engine seized. I quickly reset the trimming tabs, turned off the petrol cocks and put the aircraft into a gentle glide. We broke wireless silence to send out an 'SOS' giving our position.

As we descended through the haze, strangely free from the noise of engines, it became apparent that the island we had seen was, in fact, one of a group. By this time we were near the water and all my attention was concentrated on carrying out the forced landing. My Navigator/Bomb Aimer, Sergeant Podger, and my Wireless Operator/Air Gunner, Leading Aircraftsman Martin, had taken up their emergency ditching positions aft and I manoeuvred the aircraft so that we should land on the sea 250-300 yards from the shore, heading towards a narrow beach. Holding off as long as possible, I felt the tail of the aircraft cleave the waves and I hauled hard back on the control column, feeling the crippled craft sink deeper into the sea. We might have skated nicely on the beach but, while still some 200 yards from the shore, the aircraft was suddenly impaled on submerged coral and stopped dead. A heavy swell was running and an avalanche of water crashed in through the opened hatch above my head. We got the dinghy overboard and started to paddle for the shore but soon found that the tide race was carrying us further out to sea. Clambering over the side, we swam the 200 yards to the beach, pulling the dinghy behind us, and fell exhausted on the sands.

We silently thanked God for our deliverance.

It was now three o'clock in the afternoon and nothing had passed our lips since dawn. Fortunately, our injuries were slight but we were hungry and parched and our first thought was to find water. Our emergency rations had gone to the bottom of the sea when the belly of the aircraft had been ripped open; even if these had been recoverable, we did not feel like going back into the turbulent waters. The aircraft, by this time disintegrating under the continual sawing motion on the jagged reef, had almost disappeared beneath the waves.

But we were by no means worried about the situation as our 'SOS' signal had been acknowledged by base and we thought it would be only a matter of hours before a ship or flying boat would appear to our rescue.

The island we had landed on appeared to be roughly four miles long by about two miles across, rising steeply from the shore to a height of some 800 feet and covered with thick jungle down to the water's edge. The coastline was made up of small sandy beaches, bounded by huge boulders and mangrove. At high tide, the sea came almost to the edge of the jungle.

We probed into the undergrowth in search of water and found a brackish pond which relieved our thirst. This pond was at the top of the very beach on which we had landed; it was remarkable that, in all our subsequent explorations, we found no other water fit to drink. We searched for food but found only one fruit-bearing tree, which we could not identify, but its fruit was extremely bitter; so we preferred to remain hungry, thinking it would only be a matter of hours before we were picked up.

It was getting late in the afternoon and it seemed probable that our rescue would not be affected until the following day, so we set about collecting wood to build a fire. Fortunately our matches had dried in the hot sun and we soon had a blazing fire going. We built up a stack of wood to keep it replenished during the night, partly because we were uncertain of the animal life on the island, but mainly as a beacon to guide our rescuers. We settled ourselves down to sleep and took it in turns to keep watch – one hour's watch, two hours' sleep.

The blazing fire threw strange shadows into the jungle now awakened for its nocturnal cacophony, the shrillness of millions of insects providing a deafening background for the strange squawks and grunts of unseen animals. Occasionally the light of the fire would be reflected in a pair of burning eyes which peered out of the undergrowth, and then as quickly disappeared. The soothing wash of the waves, now quieted after the turmoil of the day, lapped gently on the shore.

The welcome dawn brought warmth to our chilled bodies and we set about collecting fuel to build up the fire to aid our rescuers who must surely be close at hand. We searched for anything in the way of food but it was incredible how, with profuse vegetation abounding, there was nothing fit for human consumption.

This was in the days when the art of survival on the sea and in the jungle had not had the specialist study it later received, when all aircrew carried their own survival kits and dinghies were elaborately provisioned. As it was, we had nothing except the dinghy, two distress rockets and the tattered clothes we stood up in. We wrote 'SOS' with leaves and branches in 10 feet letters in the sand and sat in the shade of the jungle to escape the blistering sun, awaiting our rescuers.

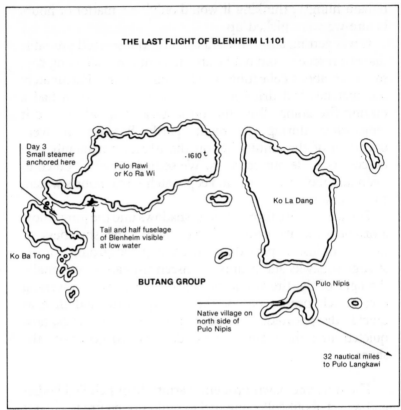

THE LAST FLIGHT OF BLENHEIM L1101

Day 3
Small steamer
anchored here

Pulo Rawi
or Ko Ra Wi

.1610 t

Ko La Dang

Tail and half fuselage
of Blenheim visible
at low water

Ko Ba Tong

BUTANG GROUP

Pulo Nipis

Native village on
north side of
Pulo Nipis

32 nautical miles
to Pulo Langkawi

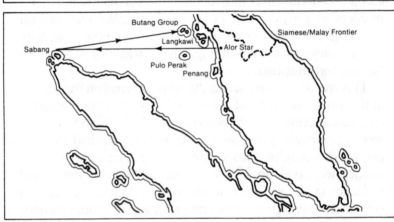

Butang Group

Siamese/Malay Frontier

Langkawi

Alor Star

Sabang

Pulo Perak

Penang

18

In the afternoon, two ships appeared on the horizon – warships apparently, judging by their wide superstructure. We made smoke signals with wet leaves and at dusk built up the fire into a huge blaze. After dark we fired one of the distress rockets; the other was still wet and just fizzled like a damp squib. We thought they must have seen our signals and would pick us up in the morning.

Discussing the trend of events that evening, we thought it rather strange that no aircraft had appeared during the day as we knew that the immediate action taken on our 'SOS' signal would have been to send out aircraft to search for us. And the doubt came into our minds whether the island we were on was the one we named in our emergency signal. Our charts had been lost in the crash landing but when Podger recalled that the name of the island he had passed to Martin for radio transmission was 'Pulo Perak' I was startled; I knew that Pulo Perak was an isolated rock rising sheer out of the sea, midway between Malaya and Sumatra, over a hundred miles from the nearest land, an impossible place on which to make a forced landing. I had flown to this pin-point in the sea on navigational exercises and I remembered it quite distinctly. This island we were on, one of a group, was obviously not Pulo Perak, and it became only too clear that the search which was undoubtedly being carried out in the Pulo Perak area would report 'No trace' and we should be given up as lost. Our otherwise cheerful spirits were somewhat dampened as the sombre truth, with all its possible consequences, sank in.

One could not blame Podger for misreading our position on the chart as, coming down through the thick haze, in the tenseness of the last few moments, he naturally thought that the island for which we were heading was Pulo Perak an island which was, in fact, almost on our true track. We found out later that the island we were on was actually 60 miles north by east of Pulo Perak. It was, therefore, not to be wondered at that the search in progress did not extend as far as the group of islands on which we were stranded. In any case, as captain of the aircraft the responsibility was mine and, in normal circumstances, I would have checked the position.

Another disturbing thought came to mind: we knew that by this time casualty signals would have been sent out to our next-of-kin reporting us as 'missing'. Our fervent hope was that we should be rescued within the next few days before the final and fatal signal 'missing believed killed' would be despatched.

Nevertheless we were alive and we laughed and joked the evening away. We built up our fire and turned in, continuing our watches throughout the night.

The third day dawned bringing with it renewed hope.

We were now 48 hours without food and felt the pangs of hunger. We wandered along the beach collecting wood and each ate of the fruit we had previously found; but it was extremely sour and the consequences were painful. We tried several types of leaves but they were bitter and most unappetising.

Our explorations had convinced us that the island was uninhabited but there were signs that it had been lived on at some time or other. From the remains of an atap shelter and stakes in the water it appeared that it might have been used as a periodical fishing ground. This was a comforting thought, the main conjecture being when next it would be visited.

About mid day our spirits soared as out to sea a small coastal steamer came into view and anchored off an island separated from us by a channel about a mile wide.

We threw wet leaves on the fire and soon clouds of smoke were billowing up. We tried to light our second rocket but it was still too wet to ignite. We hurried along the beach to get to the point nearest the steamer, clambering over the rocks along the coastline, saturated with spray and swimming round the rocky promontories, heedless of the cuts inflicted by the submerged coral.

The Author in Parachute Training Hangar at RAF Abingdon, 1956

The late Squadron Leader ASK Scarf, VC, at RAF Scampton, 1936. Heyford aircraft in the background. Known to his friends as 'Pongo' he refused to take life seriously, was always full of fun and ready for a party. He was awarded the only VC in the fall of Singapore

The driving force which enabled me to return to Britain after being shot down at Annecy in France on the night of 15 August 1943, WAAF Ruth Fuller

Officers Mess ablutions 1939, Queens Royal Regiment, Allahabad. Unchanged since the days of the Mutiny. Flying Officer Stephens, 62 Squadron, takes a bath

At last we reached the point where we were directly opposite the steamer, though still separated by over a mile of water. We waved our shirts and shouted, tried to light another fire on the spot but the wind was too strong for our few remaining matches. There was no sign of recognition from the ship although we could vaguely discern the movements of human beings on board.

Martin said he would go on to reach narrower waters and swim across the channel but I forbade him to do this as the strong tide running between the island would have made the attempt most hazardous. He went on, I caught him and expressly ordered him not to go, but he slipped from my grasp and disappeared round the promontory.

After an interminable time, weakened by shouting and with our eyes glued to the steamer, we perceived more smoke coming from the funnel and it slowly pulled away from its anchorage. It was turning in a wide arc and coming straight towards us! Here at last was our salvation. We leapt madly upon the rocks and shouted until we were hoarse.

But the turning circle of the steamer continued – we were frantic in our excitement – and it pulled away, ignoring us, and disappeared from sight among the islands. Our spirits just about touched rock bottom; but my main concern was what had happened to Martin. We waited for a time and then, leaving Podger, I went on to look for him. Across the narrow beaches, crawling round the rocky promontories, I went on to a point beyond which I felt he would not have gone, but there was no sign of him. I wandered slowly back, greatly distressed in the thought that he had undoubtedly perished in his gallant attempt to swim across the channel. I found Podger sitting disconsolately on the beach. There was no need to tell him I had not found Martin; he must have read it in my face.

I decided that we ought to return to our camp as there was no point in waiting. With the tide rising, we would be hard pressed to get back before darkness fell; and we had to return as our only source of drinking water was on that beach. Before we left, we wrote in large letters in the sand: 'Martin – return to camp.' It was all we could do.

The sun had set by the time we got back. We assuaged our thirst with the brackish water and collected sufficient wood to keep the fire going during the night. We had been resting for about an hour when out of the shadows loomed a figure and – heaven be praised – Martin staggered in. We were overjoyed at being together again and his return cleared the despondency from our hearts. Poor fellow, he was almost all in; he told us he had attempted to swim across the narrows but that the tide had been too strong for him and it was all he could do to regain the shore. It was a very gallant attempt.

We were all too tired to keep watch that night so slept where we lay, each replenishing the fire as he woke from fitful sleep during the night.

A heavy mist had enveloped us during the dark hours and we woke at dawn on this fourth day, cold and stiff with the dampness in our bones.

The hunger pains in our stomachs had receded but we were now beginning to feel physically weak. The brackish water kept us alive. We often lay in the shallow waters as a relief from the hard sand, absorbing the life sustaining salt into our bodies. We continued to collect dead wood for our fire, but each excursion sent us further afield which taxed our diminishing strength. The various leaves we sampled were revoltingly inedible. Our feet had swollen so much that we could not wear shoes and the cuts in our feet picked up the burning sand. During the heat of the day we lay beneath the trees but we got little rest from the millions of ants and swarms of flies which bit into the flesh and drew blood.

I was beginning to feel worried about Podger; he did not seem to have got over the disappointment of the steamer episode and would sit for hours without saying a word or wander off along the beach. We did our best to cheer him up but it was obvious that he was beginning to feel the strain. We had begun to build a large beacon of dried wood and leaves to be lit at the opportune moment and, whilst it was essential to conserve one's strength as far as possible, Podger would attack this task with such ferocity of purpose that within a short time he would become exhausted, leaving him more morose than before.

At low tide, we set out along the beach further afield than we had been before when, rounding a promontory, we saw a village in the distance with washing out to dry! We hurried towards it, our flagging spirits revived; but the hallucination turned out to be a group of rocks and the 'washing' was the white sand gleaming behind the mangroves. We arrived back in camp late in the afternoon and soon the sun dropped below the horizon and the chill night air enveloped us.

We huddled together beside the fire and fell into uneasy sleep.

The warm sun at dawn awoke us on the fifth morning, seeping into our bones and bringing new hope for the day. But there was no doubt that our strength was greatly reduced and it was as much as we could do to collect wood for the fire.

Again smoke appeared on the horizon but it came no nearer.

Podger persevered with the beacon which was now about eight feet high, whilst Martin and I forced our way into the jungle on another search for food. It was hard going and after an hour we had only made about a hundred yards headway. It was infuriating that, with all the hum of nature about us, there was nothing to be found which was edible. We occasionally saw a large iguana dart back into the undergrowth and we could hear the chattering of monkeys high in the trees; a glorious tropical bird would flit across through the branches above, but all were out of our grasp.

Back on the beach a few tiny crabs had come up for air, but they were quick to dart back into their holes. The few we caught we masticated, spitting out the gritty bits. Perhaps our ears were playing us false, but we thought we heard an aircraft behind us, on the other side of the island; but it never appeared.

In the afternoon there was a particularly low tide and the tail of the aircraft appeared above the surface of the gentle swell. Martin and I waded out through the coral outcrop and clambered on board. We salvaged the Lewis gun and two pans of ammunition, thinking they might come in useful as a sound signal, and also a fabric engine cover which we later dried in the sun and used as a blanket.

The swift setting of the sun brought to a close another day. It was obvious that Podger was now feeling the accumulated strain and I feared that he might become unbalanced. The burning sun and lack of food had drained our reserves of strength considerably and our bones showed up through the taut skin. I realised that our situation was becoming serious, though no doubt we could survive several more days sustained by the brackish water. But the sooner we were rescued the better, particularly for Podger's sake, before our overtaxed hearts suffered any permanent impairment. Somehow, even in these near-desperate circumstances, I could not believe that we were destined to rot on this island, but that help would reach us before too late.

Pulling the engine cover over us, grateful for its protection from damp night air, we drifted into uneasy sleep.

It rained heavily during the night and we welcomed the rising of the sun on this sixth morning, absorbing its warmth into our aching bodies.

We set about our daily task of collecting wood, but it was a slow process as any effort made our hearts thump and the weakness of our limbs necessitated frequent rests.

We lay in the shade of the jungle and stripped the Lewis gun, cleaned it as best we could after its five days immersion in sea water and reassembled it. We had fitted a round into the breach when . . . a boat came silently round the edge of the mangrove, heading for our beach. We were spellbound and looked again, fearful of another hallucination. But yes! It was a boat! A small native fishing boat with human beings on board! Podger snatched up the Lewis gun but I wrenched it from him and threw it into the undergrowth. We didn't speak; we didn't want to frighten them away.

Stepping out onto the beach, we walked slowly down towards the shore, waving timidly. And then, gaining courage as the vessel still continued in our direction, we broke into a trot, strange noises came from our throats and we dashed into the water and hauled the boat up to the water's edge.

The Malay fishermen were as astonished to see us as we were overjoyed to see them. They couldn't understand these strange wild-looking Europeans shaking them by the hand and hugging them, laughing hysterically and dragging them up the beach.

When the first frantic wave of excitement was spent, we attempted to explain to them how we came to be there. But it was difficult to make them understand in the few words of Malay which we knew. I remembered the words for aeroplane – 'kapal terbang' – ship of the air, and Podger produced from an RAF diary a photograph of an aircraft, still fairly discernable despite frequent immersions in salt water. With much sign language depicting our crash and pointing out the tail of our aircraft just visible above the waves, we tried to explain to them the reason for our presence on the island. Gradually they began to understand and there was much consternation amongst them – a wizened old man, his elderly son and three small boys.

We let them get over their surprise and then I said 'Mau makan – tida makan anam hari' meaning we needed food as we hadn't eaten for six days. Without delay the old man spoke to the boys who went back to the boat and returned with a large cauldron of rice which they placed on our fire to heat up.

Then they fetched a basket of what looked like ping-pong balls but which we learned were turtles' eggs; these they put on to boil in a separate vessel of water.

We endeavoured to carry on a conversation but could hardly wait until the meal was cooked. The smell of the hot rice tickled our nostrils and permeated our empty stomachs. Meanwhile the boys had brought up from the boat several green coconuts; with deft slashes of a hatchet they cut off the tops so that we could drink the delicious milk, ice cold and tasting like nectar.

When the meal was cooked the old man, producing small china bowls, served us with rice and showed us how to nip the soft shell of the turtle's egg to get at the yolk, a hard yellow ball. We ate until our shrunken stomachs were distended, washed down with the delicious coconut milk.

Without any doubt, the finest meal we had ever had in our lives.

Then the old man produced some native cigarettes, thick reeds about six inches long packed with tobacco. We gratefully accepted his offer to smoke but the strong weed in our weakened condition set our heads reeling.

During our difficult conversation, I had been endeavouring to find out where we were and to make the old man understand that we wanted to be taken back to Alor Star, Kedah, on the coast of Malaya. I gathered that we were on an island called Pulo Rawi, but, without our charts, this did not convey very much. And to the fishermen, the name Alor Star and Kedah didn't seem to mean much either. I handed the old man a Malayan $5 note to signify our intention of rewarding him, but he just turned it over in his hands and passed it over to his son to inspect. It was very obvious that they had never seen paper money before.

The old man kept his eye on the sun and, towards mid-day, signified that we should leave. We were only too glad to get away from this island which had so nearly become our grave, feeling fortified in strength and spirit, we helped them carry their utensils to the boat and climbed aboard.

The boat was about twenty feet in length, similar to the koleh we ourselves had sailed in Singapore waters, but with eight of us aboard it was down to the gunwales. The single sail was raised and the balancing board pushed out to the windward side, along which one of the young boys scooted with the agility of a monkey. Fortunately, the sea was calm and the breeze, filling the sail, carried us away from the inhospitable island of Rawi.

We sailed through the group of islands (the Butang Group) and at sunset approached another island, the most easterly in the group, called Pulo Nipis, where there was a fishing village above the shore.

All the inhabitants, about a hundred all told, came out to see the strange catch the old fisherman had brought back with him. From the cool reception we received, it was not possible to glean the intentions of these primitive people as they led us to a hut raised on piles above the ground. There was much murmuring amongst them; but we felt a certain amount of re-assurance when they produced food – rice and dried fish and more of the deliciously fresh coconut milk.

As darkness fell, a ferocious-looking individual came into the hut without a word and lit a small oil burning lamp; but they left us to ourselves and, settling down on the rush-covered floor, we were soon asleep.

We awoke with a start during the night when a drum started booming; but a few minutes later it ceased and, after waiting in silence for some time, we returned to uneasy sleep.

The soft light of dawn filtered through the bamboo walls of our hut and we took stock of our surroundings.

The single room was about ten feet square by six feet high and was completely bare except for a framed print of some brown gentleman in what appeared to be an admiral's uniform, highly coloured in the eastern style, which hung on one of the walls. We tried to decipher the hieroglyphics which surrounded the portrait but we could not recognise it as Malay script. An emblem surmounted the picture and it dawned on us that this must be the badge of Siam.

If this meant that we were on a Siamese island, our troubles were not yet over as Siam was still a neutral country and we were in imminent danger of being interned! Our discussion was interrupted by the door being thrust open and a native entered bearing a tray of rice and dried fish and three vessels of weak tea. Shortly afterwards about twenty fierce-looking Malays crowded into the room and squatted down, filling the room to overflowing.

I tried to convey to them our thanks for their hospitality, food and shelter, although my vocabulary was very limited. Not one of them could understand a word of English. Then I attempted to convey to them that we would like them to take us to Alor Star but I gleaned from their murmurings amongst themselves that they were not keen on this idea. I persevered, a few more Malay words coming into my head and told them that they would be paid for their services. I mentioned a sum of 'anam puloh ringgit' – why $60 I cannot remember as this was the equivalent of £7 sterling, a very cheap ransom for the return of three fully-trained aircrew! But it obviously seemed a lot of money to them and at least we had reached some basis for discussion.

I could not get over their reluctance to take us to the mainland; and then it struck me that, if we were, in fact on a Siamese island, they would probably be reluctant to land us on 'foreign' territory. They kept mentioning the name 'Pulo Taratau' – another island according to the prefix 'Pulo' – but this name meant nothing to us. I tried to visualise the map and came to the conclusion that we were probably north of the international boundary line and that Taratau was another island laying between our present position and the mainland of Malaya; and, not recognising the name Taratau, was also more than likely to be Siamese territory. We had to avoid being taken there at all costs as there we should without doubt run into Siamese officialdom, more pro-Axis than pro-British, with certain internment to follow.

Concentrating on the map forming in my mind, I remembered that Langkawi, a large island settlement some thirty miles west of Alor Star, was just south of the international boundary line – in fact, the international boundary runs between Taratau and Langkawi which are separated by a channel some 5 miles wide – and so I decided to switch my argument in favour of being taken to Langkawi, British territory, which would not necessitate such a long sea voyage for our rescuers.

When I mentioned the name Langkawi, it was immediately apparent that the island was known to them. At last we were getting somewhere; but they were still reluctant to agree and persisted in their intention to take us to Pulo Taratau.

The argument went on throughout the morning. The atmosphere of the hut became stifling with so many beings crammed into the confined space but, although my body was wilting, I was determined to overcome this last obstacle to freedom. I concentrated on the 'anam puloh ringgit' they would receive, and tried to make it clear that we should not be welcomed on Pulo Taratau.

At last, after hours of wrangling, they finally agreed to take us to Langkawi. Our hearts leapt with joy and relief. Soon we should be back amongst our own folk and, even more important, be able to announce our survival to our grief-stricken families at home who, without doubt, had by now received the fatal signal.

We were given another meal and at mid-day were escorted down the beach to a sea-going sampan, a 35-foot open boat already manned by her crew of five. We said goodbye to our benefactors, now more friendly, and waved to the villagers gathered on the beach to see us off. The large single bamboo-laced sail was hoisted up the mast and, with a following breeze, we turned our backs on Pulo Nipis, a further step towards civilisation.

As the sun sank behind us in the west, the faint outline of an island appeared on the darkening horizon ahead and we sailed on into the night. The breeze freshened and the sampan buried her bows in the swell, throwing up a beautiful phosphorescence in her wake. The deck boards were painful to our protruding bones but the joy in our hearts transcended any physical discomfort that we suffered.

The first glimmer of dawn silhouetted an island before us. A certain amount of anxiety remained as we could not be quite sure that the Malays would adhere to their bargain but, as the sun rose, the outline of the island brought the final relief to our fears as we recognised the wooded hills of Langkawi.

With the tying up of the boat against the wooden jetty at the village settlement of Kuah our tribulations were over. I clambered up on to the landing stage and tottered ashore. I saw the Union Jack flying from a tall flagstaff outside Government buildings, went in and announced myself to a startled District Officer. Briefly I told him our story and sought permission to send off signals announcing our return. He placed a pad and pencil on the desk before me and I wrote out my message stating that we had been picked up uninjured and well.

This culminating action after the trials and tribulations of the past seven days, snapped the last thread of my resistance; the dam burst within me and I wept. I was glad Podger and Martin were not in the room to witness this moment of weakness.'

CHAPTER 3

The Humble
shall be Exalted

Dai Jones had been driven out of his beloved South Wales
by the depression in the thirties. He joined the RAF and after
initial training he was posted to one of the squadrons at RAF
Cranfield in Bedfordshire in the rank of AC2 (Airman 2nd
Class) and the trade of ACH (Aircrafthand). His status was
'the lowest form of life' in the RAF.

Being as yet unskilled he could only be employed on simple
tasks such as cleaning aircraft and brushing out the hangar.
He was however willing, popular and a splendid rugby player
and these attributes lifted him out of the rut of ordinary
mortals. As a scrum half he was superb but when it came to
working with aeroplanes he was undoubtedly a menace for he
was ham handed and accident prone.

His first unfortunate encounter with aircraft came when,
overkeen to put the chocks to the wheels of a Hart, he was
struck a glancing blow on the head by a still-spinning
propeller. Few men survive this type of accident but, being
Dai, he was only stunned.

His next misfortune was to crush his foot between hangar
doors as they were being closed. As the doors weighed 50 tons
each he was lucky to break only a couple of toes.

Back at work after convalescing, he was helping a pilot to
put on his straps when he stepped smartly backwards and put
his foot through the fabric of the lower mainplane. Enough

was enough. His squadron commander banished him to the cookhouse. Within a week he had caught his hand in the bread slicer.

His squadron commander, an understanding man, pointed out that so far he had been a liability to the Service and asked him whether there was anything he could do without making a hash of it.

'Yes, sir', said Dai eagerly. 'I'd like to be on the coal permanent.'

Now in the pre-war Air Force this was a most unpopular fatigue, usually allocated to each squadron in turn, who supplied men weekly for the coal party. The coal party had to bag the coal from bulk, load the bags on to a lorry and distribute them to sections, messes and married quarters round the camp.

It was a dirty, sometimes cold and unrewarding fatigue, avoided if possible. That Dai should want to go 'on the coal' was a welcome surprise.

And so to the coal party he went - permanent. Everyone was happy, Dai because he was dealing with a substance which generations of his family had dealt with, the squadron commander because Dai was working well away from the aeroplanes, and the station because they had at last achieved continuity, in that at least one member of the coal party was permanent.

The wives in married quarters got to know Dai and liked him. He knew their children's names, he was always cheerful and his perambulations round the camp were accompanied by much chit-chat and tea-drinking. He had found his niche. But fate decreed that he should be posted to the Far East, where his history was unknown, where he found there was no coal to distribute but where circumstances were to elevate him to a position of great respect.

War started soon after he arrived in Singapore. There, his previous misfortunes unknown, he was put in charge of a small party of locally employed chinese labourers who worked in a servicing hangar at unskilled jobs such as brushing floors and polishing aircraft.

Now a Walrus single engined amphibian had been taken into the servicing hangar for a major overhaul. A particularly good job was made of this aircraft and she finally emerged for testing, beautifully painted in her new wartime camouflage.

After her ground running tests she was handed over to one of the pilots for flight testing. With a fitter to accompany him, they clambered aboard and carried out the usual procedures, including testing the flying controls and boost and revolutions of the engine at full throttle.

He was satisfied that everything was correct, so chocks were waved away and they taxied out to the downwind side of the airfield. Take-off was to be towards the Johore Strait, whose waters lapped the airfield edge. With the sun shining and a nice ten-knot breeze blowing the pilot opened the throttle and the Walrus trundled forward. Rather slowly, the pilot thought, but then he was starting up rising ground – the grass-covered airfield was dome-shaped to get rid of tropical rain – and he consoled himself that she would soon get a move on once she topped the rise. Over the top of the dome her speed did increase, but she still did not wish to leave the ground.

Round the airfield perimeter was a large ditch, six feet across at the top and four feet deep. This was to collect the rains, but it also acted as a wonderful trap to stop aeroplanes which still had their wheels on the ground.

With the ditch only a few feet away and a mere 50 knots on the clock, the pilot heaved the stick back and the Walrus lurched into the air in a semi-stalled condition. She was now over the water and to help reduce drag the pilot yelled at the fitter to pump up the wheels; it made little difference. The aircraft refused to gain height and was indeed still flying in a semi-stalled condition. Yet the engine revolutions and the boost-guage showed that the power of the engine was at its maximum.

The pilot realised that he had insufficient flying speed to attempt a turn and that any attempt to do so would result in his falling into the Johore Strait on his side. Beyond the strait the ground rose rapidly and he certainly couldn't climb enough to get over it. He had only one alternative - to land her on the water, which the Walrus, being an amphibian, was well able to do. It wasn't necessary to reduce the throttle setting to land. She flopped on to the water just as he was thinking about it.

He couldn't imagine what was wrong. He had flown her before she went in for her inspection. He was getting the same engine power as then and yet she didn't want to fly.

He taxied back downwind for half a mile and then turned into wind again and tried his magnetos on a fast run-up. He opened the engine up to full power. Again he got full revolutions and boost, but the Walrus showed no desire to leave the water.

In disgust he cut the throttle and taxied back to the flying-boat slip. Lowering the wheels he put her at the slip and she taxied out of the water in her usual duck-like attitude.

RAF technicians possess a kind of telepathy which tells them when something is wrong and so it was on this occasion, for they appeared like flies. The lesser mortals looked on while the pilot, a flight sergeant and several senior technicians discussed the phenomenon with much gesticulating and hand-waving. It was hot and nearly midday and finally the order was given to push the Walrus into the hangar and everyone packed up for tiffin.

In the ante-room at the officers mess various theories were advanced as to why the Walrus wouldn't fly and the technical officers came in for their fair share of leg-pulling.

As it was the Far-East, there was no work in the afternoon, but the next morning at break of day the Walrus was pushed out of the hangar again and checked. Once more the boost of the engine and the revolutions obtained were not only enough but slightly in excess of the requirements. It could only be one thing – the rigging of the wings.

So back in the hangar went the aircraft for a rigging check. It was finished by midday, but too late for an air test, so once more the technical officers had to run the gauntlet of the inevitable leg-pulling in the mess.

Day three dawned with the Walrus on the tarmac, the rigging perfect, and the engine boost increased slightly over the stipulated amount. The air was cool and therefore more lift should be available.

The pilot taxied out. This time she would definitely fly. No aircraft could have had greater attention paid to her.

With a vast crowd surreptitiously watching, she sped across the air field . . . and the same thing happened! Only by a miracle did she clear the perimeter ditch and again the pilot put her down on the water.

It was a very glum party which greeted him as he taxied up the slip.

In the mess at lunch the atmosphere had changed. The Walrus was no longer a joke and the technical officers kept to themselves at one end of the ante-room.

Next day the boost-gauge and rev-counter were tested and calibrated and found to be perfect. In the officers' mess it was more than a pilot's life was worth to ask a technical officer how the Walrus was going on. Technical security was perfect. The matter was not for discussion except on a 'need to know' basis.

Now it had been Dai's duty to clean the Walrus regularly before it was dismantled for its major servicing and while his team of coolies polished the hull Dai would clamber up on to the fuselage and lovingly polish the engine. He wasn't afraid of engines when they weren't running.

On this day, the fifth, he had started to wipe down the engine when he suddenly clambered down and presented himself to the Flight Sergeant with the request that he might have an interview with the Senior Technical Officer.

Not unnaturally the Flight Sergeant wanted to know why,

but Dai wouldn't say. The Flight Sergeant was adamant that unless Dai told him the reason why he wanted an interview, he just wouldn't be granted one.

Now Dai had discovered why the Walrus wouldn't fly, and he realised that the man making this discovery would be esteemed throughout the station, indeed throughout the island, for the woes of the Walrus had spread to other stations.

He also knew the habit of NCOs to bring glory on themselves at other people's expense if they had the opportunity. He had been in the Service long enough to appreciate that if he was to reap the full benefit of his discovery, he and he alone must tell the STO why the aircraft wouldn't fly.

The Flight Sergeant was a reasonable man and Dai, although not regarded as a member of the intelligentsia, was a popular chap, so in the end, the Flight Sergeant agreed to ask the STO if he would see him.

'I hear you want to see me, Jones,' said the STO as Dai was marched in, 'and you won't tell the Flight Sergeant what it is about.'

'That's right, Sir,' said Dai.

'Well, do you wish to speak with me with the Flight Sergeant present? If it's personal I'll ask him to withdraw if you wish.'

'I don't mind the Flight Sergeant being present now, Sir,' replied Dai. 'I just wanted to tell you that I know the reason why the Walrus won't fly.'

With the lowest form of life in the Air Force, an aircraft-hand, broaching such a delicate subject to the Senior Technical Officer, it would have been an understatement to say that the atmosphere could have been cut with a knife.

The STO's face went red. The Flight Sergeant was longing to get Dai on his own and tell him what he thought of him.

'And why, Jones, won't the Walrus fly?' asked the STO in

a 'Sam, pick-up-thee-musket' tone of voice.

'Because, Sir, the propeller is on back to front.'

And so it was. And that was the cause of all the trouble and the reason why, on every Walrus propeller from 1939 onwards, the word 'Aft' was painted on the boss of each of the twin wooden blades which went to make up the four-bladed pusher propeller.

But why did Dai discover something which others more highly trained were unable to spot?

It so happened that the leading edge of all wooden propellers used to have a brass strip to protect them from hail encountered in flight. Dai knew that his cleaning rag caught in these brass protection strips when he rubbed the leading edge. He therefore always ran his rag down the trailing edge which was smooth, but on this occasion his rag jammed, caught in the brass strip!

'Funny,' he thought. Then it dawned on him that the prop was on back to front.

CHAPTER 4

Don't argue
with the Slipstream

About a year and a half before flying out to Singapore I had been sent on a one-week parachute packing course at RAF Manston. This presumably was to prepare me for an ancillary duty such as officer in charge of Parachute Section. At the end of the course in a fit of enthusiasm I applied to carry out a parachute jump. I forgot all about this indiscretion until a year later when, one morning, Harley Boxall, our adjutant at that time said 'Your parachute jump has come up. You'd better get yourself over to Henlow right away. The Squadron Commander says you can take a Hind but you'd better take someone with you to fly the kite back in case you bend yourself!' So I didn't matter! It was the aeroplane that was important.

I persuaded Norman Irving to come with me and off we flew to Henlow on a cold and frosty morning. A weak sun illuminated the Bedfordshire countryside.

Pre-war parachuting was in a very primitive state. The parachutist did not travel inside the fuselage and then jump through a commodious hole or open doorway but was required to stand on the wing tip of a Virginia biplane bomber from before taxi-ing to the moment of dropping.

At Henlow a Virginia stood menacingly on the tarmac the brass and copperwork on the engines shining in the sunlight. There was a small platform at the base of the rear strut on each wingtip. In order to equalise the drag two parachutists had to be carried and had to stand on these platforms and be pulled off at exactly the same time. I learnt that my companion in misfortune was another volunteer, Pilot Officer Lovett.

We were fitted with parachutes and briefed. 'You will mount the ladder and step on to the platforms. You will not wear gloves. We don't want any fumbling. You will face aft. The slipstream will blow you against the strut. Don't worry about falling off. It is practically impossible to do so due to the slipstream. After you get to 2000 feet the pilot will throttle back. When the reargunner stands up in his turret and circles both his hands above his head you will release the strut with your right hand and grip the 'D' ring of the ripcord and then, holding the strut with your left hand, you will step round to the other side. It will take some strength to hold on with one hand. Whatever happens you are not to take your right hand off the ripcord. When you have positioned yourself on the rearside of the strut watch the front gunner. As you approach the airfield he will stand up and hold both arms above his head. When he drops his arms you are to pull the ripcord; a small point but the ripcords are on the inventory and cost fifteen shillings so don't drop them if they pull right out of their housing. Don't attempt to stand on your feet when landing; just crumple up and roll over if you can. Oh Griffiths, your chute is by way of being experimental. The rigging lines are longer on one side than the other. We are hoping that this modification may damp out oscillation as you descend so don't worry if the canopy looks one sided'.

We waddled out to the aircraft like a couple of Muscovy Ducks in lay and then mounted the scaffolds. Had Charles the First felt like this? Oh why had I filled in that application form?

The take off was shattering. The briefing officer was right. There was no arguing with the slipstream and you couldn't fall off if you tried. It was odd standing on the waving wing tip as the aircraft rumbled across the grass airfield and rather frightening as the first hedges went by underneath. The Napier Lion engines roared away and I couldn't help but recall that the flight-path of a Virginia on one engine was like the proverbial brick.

The engines throttled back. The moment of truth had arrived.

The reargunner stood up in his pulpit and with a signal like an ecclesiastical benediction he rotated his raised arms. This was the hardest part. It was icy cold and both my hands were frozen but at least I made sure that I had hold of the ripcord. Once I was facing forward it was all I could do to hold on to the strut with my left hand. The front gunner with his back to the slipstream was holding his hands high and looking backwards over his shoulder to determine the right moment to give the signal. At last he dropped his hands. I couldn't have held on any longer anyway so I pulled the ripcord and was pleasantly surprised to find that all the noise and wind had gone and I was swinging underneath my fully developed canopy. I still had the 'D' ring and ripcord in my hand! At least the inventory would be correct! It was a very pleasant way to be parachuted and not so frightening as todays 'jump into space.'

Lovett landed alongside the London and North Eastern Railway line just inside the airfield boundary. I 'crumpled up' as briefed but on the tarmac. It was hard and it was some time before I could stand up.

After the inevitable cup of tea I felt better and flew the Hind back to Cranfield but I'd certainly done something to my back.

It played up once or twice that summer and finally flared up in Singapore. From the 1939 Christmas onwards I was a sick man off and on and finally a medical board invalided me back to the UK. I sailed for home in the SS Talma on 29th April 1940.

At the time this seemed the worst moment in my life.

Classified 'Unfit for flying duties', repatriated and leaving 62 Squadron and my friends after 3 years. But man proposes and God disposes. Had I not had back trouble I would probably have ended up in a grave alongside the Burma railway.

Leaving my bosom friends Hutch and Pongo was the most unpalatable part of the posting back home. Hutch I was to see once more. He got away from Malaya only to die on 'D' Day towing a glider. Pongo was soon to die in Malaya in particularly sad circumstances and to become the 'unknown VC of the Far East.'

It is said that there are seven qualities required of a pilot which no written exam can reveal. They are sense of responsibility, leadership, anticipation, resourcefulness, hardihood, courage and ability to get on with people.

Pongo possessed all these qualities and more but maintained a facade which delighted his friends and irritated his seniors for he pretended that he was a bit 'dim' and that all orders, complex navigational problems and technicalities of aircraft were beyond him. It was all an act as his peers well knew. He was however unlucky at times which gave his superiors the impression that he didn't take life seriously enough.

He was frequently late for lectures and generally made morning parades by the skin of his teeth dashing on to the parade ground just as the command 'Fall in the Officers' was given.

He did this on one formal parade and took up his position in front of his flight. Prayers were said and then the Station Commander left the saluting base to carry out his inspection to find Pongo standing stiffly to attention, immaculately turned out but instead of his regulation service black tie he was wearing a Richmond Rowing Club tie! A late night party, no breakfast and dressing in too much of a hurry caused this peccadillo.

When the Japanese attack came in December 1941, 62

41

Squadron were at Alor Star where they were strafed by the Japanese while fuelling and bombing up. Some of the aircraft were patched up and flown down to Butterworth where they were prepared for a late afternoon raid on the Japanese occupied base of Singora in Siam. Pongo took off first and was about to do a circuit so that the rest of the squadron could catch up and formate on him. But as he looked down he saw the remainder of the aircraft disintegrate. A high level formation of Japanese bombers had bombed at the moment he left the airfield. He could justifiably have cancelled his mission and landed elsewhere but he pressed on and alone bombed Singora at low level, his reargunner Flight Sergeant Rich getting some excellent shooting into rows of parked Jap aircraft. Jap fighters however were soon on to the doomed Blenheim. Flying at treetop height Pongo jinked his way back to Alor Star but his left arm was shattered and bullets had smashed his back. Rich had to leave his turret and hold him back in his seat.

Paddy Calvert, the navigator, sitting alongside Pongo was able to lean across and help him with the controls. Pongo was not always fully conscious due to loss of blood and he realised that his only hope of survival was to obtain medical help quickly. By a supreme effort he summoned up the will power to carry out a flaps down wheels up landing in the rice paddy fields alongside the Alor Star hospital where his wife Sally was a nurse.

They carried him into the hospital.

In the operating theatre he squeezed Sally's hand and said 'Keep smiling Sal'. Then he died.

After $4\frac{1}{2}$ years of intensive training and having been brought to the peak of perfection this flight of Pongo's was virtually 62 Squadron's sole contribution to the war in Malaya. The remnants of the squadron got away to India where it was reformed. 'Pongo' (Squadron Leader A S K Scarf) was posthumously awarded the Victoria Cross on 21 June 1946.

It was a long journey towards home in the *SS Talma* with sick aboard from Hong Kong and Malaya. She was a very comfortable ship but her looks belied her speed. Built especially for the Far East she had two funnels because the farepaying Chinese thought that funnels meant power and speed. They worked on the principal of 'one funnel ten piecee knot'. Despite our two funnels we just managed as stately 10 knots.

When close to Eritrea, where Italian aircraft might molest us, the RAF personnel kept an aircraft watch on the flying bridge. After calling at Suez and Malta we disembarked at Marseilles on 28 May and set off in a well marked hospital train for Calais. We were still in the train 3 days later. We never did reach Calais. We saw plenty of Luftwaffe activity and eventually reached Cherbourg which had already been bombed. Those of us who could walk marched to the south of the town and spent the day near some caves overlooking the harbour. They made excellent air raid shelters. Alas there was no ship for us.

As dusk fell we were told to march down to the harbour as a ship might arrive after dark. Eventually it came – a small tug.

It is surprising how many men can get into a confined space if they stand up shoulder to shoulder and this we did all through the night, without speaking or moving. The sea was a flat calm and at dawn on 1 June we steamed into Weymouth. All baggage had been left behind in Cherbourg but by some miracle mine arrived intact in England two months later and not a thing missing!

Came a series of RAF Hospitals and then a spell at the Palace Hotel, Torquay which was a convalescent home especially for aircrew where efforts were made to get them fit again as soon as possible. Most of them had been wounded when Hitler invaded Norway and the low countries.

My future fate was decided in more ways than one at Torquay. One morning I was hobbling down the easy tread

43

main staircase. I had noticed a WAAF dusting the stairs as one notices any woman bending down and then she raised her face towards me and something went 'zing'. She had a round face, high cheekbones and blue eyes and her brown hair, obedient to RAF instructions was not only off the shoulders but, as I subsequently discovered, wound round her head like a halo, the basic structure being a silk stocking.

Up till this time I had never been seriously emotionally involved. Two things had precluded my achieving a state of matrimony. While I could give up sufficient time to go courting during the winter I found my interest waning as soon as the summer and the sailing season came around. The other preclusion was that an officer could not draw marriage allowance until he was 28 and he had to obtain permission to marry under this age. This made one stop and think and it was probably a very good restriction. However meeting Ruth Fuller, for that was her name, made me recall a remark by the Master of the Flint and Denbigh Foxhounds when he advised me some years earlier 'If you are choosing a dog, a horse or a wife go by the head; if you have any doubts then check on the Mother.' How right he was. I had no doubts even before I met the Mother for this was the woman whom I wanted to be the Mother of my children.

But it takes two to make a marriage and what had I to offer. An ex overseas General Duties Pilot unfit for flying duties who could, at times, only just hobble around.

As luck would have it Ruth's sister Daphne was also a WAAF at the Palace and friendly with another Blenheim pilot, Stuart Robertson, who was a friend of mine. Stuart, whilst strafing a German column in the low countries, had received a nine millimetre bullet and part of his armour plated seat in his right buttock. He was mending fast and although WAAFs were not supposed to mix socially with officers, regulations did not interfere with preordained events, and many successful sailing expeditions on the River Dart culminated in both Stuart and my marrying our respective WAAFs within twelve months. Poor Stuart and Daphne. Within 21 days of their marriage, as Captain of a Stirling bomber returning from operations over Germany to RAF Oakington, he was killed by a German intruder aircraft. The co-pilot managed to land the Stirling.

My fate was different, and again luck played a hand. By now my trouble was diagnosed as ankylosing spondylitis (inflammation of impacted vertebrae). On my next medical board a distinguished orthopaedic specialist, Sir Reginald Watson Jones, suggested trying one more course of treatment – deep therapy X-ray. The effect of this, in layman's language, was to burn out the marrow fat between the affected vertebrae and thus solidify the base of the spine. While it would fix the spine so that it was no longer supple it would kill the pain and strengthen it. I learnt later that it could also kill the patient by causing leukaemia if too much X-ray was given!

Whether they were getting short of pilots or not I don't know but in October 1940 I passed my medical board as fit for flying (UK only) and the repair must have been good. It allowed me to do another 4000 hours flying and to continue the things I most loved doing, ski-ing, sailing and riding.

CHAPTER 5

Boffinery

In a memorandum to the Cabinet on the 3 September 1940 Churchill stated:-

'The Navy can lose us the war but only the Air Force can win it. Therefore our supreme effort must be to gain overwhelming mastery of the air – It is by devising new weapons, and above all, by scientific leadership, that we shall best cope with the enemey's superior strength. If, for instance, the series of inventions now being developed to find and hit enemy aircraft, both from the air and from the ground, irrespective of visibility, realise what is hoped from them, not only the strategic but the munitions situation would be profoundly altered – we must regard the whole sphere of RDF* with its many refinements and measureless possibilities, as ranking in priority with the Air Force, of which it is in fact an essential part. The multiplication of the high class scientific personnel, as well as the training of those who will handle the new weapons and research work connected with them, should be the very spearpoint of our thought and effort.'

Seven weeks after this minute was written I joined this band of 'high class scientific personnel' as a humble pilot.

---

* Radar

I reported to Air Ministry (Postings) in London and was told to get weaving and go down to Christchurch near Bournemouth to join Special Duty Flight.

'What is Special Duty Flight?'

'Haven't a clue,' came the answer, 'but they want experienced Blenheim pilots. It should suit you.'

RAF Christchurch on arrival appeared more like a country cricket pitch than an aerodrome. The 'pavilion' (Duty Pilots' Hut) was a wooden hut with a verandah and hitching rail rather like a two gun saloon in the Middle West. Parked round the tiny grass airfield under the trees (Yes, trees, and aeroplanes didn't like trees!) were aircraft of various types, Battle, Anson, Hurricane, Blenheim, Fox Moth, Whitley, Spitfire and a lone United States aircraft a Boston (DB7). The majority had large toasting forks protruding from their wings and noses.

Special Duty Flight, as it was then called, provided the flying for TRE, the Telecommunications Research Establishment, which housed its scientists in laboratories on top of the cliffs at Worth Matravers near Swanage. TRE, as it was more generally known, had previously been responsible for the coastal chain of radar* stations which, by tracking the approach of German aircraft, had made victory possible in the Battle of Britain.

Research had already started into the possibility of using airborne radar (hence the toasting forks). From the Universities and from Industry were recruited not only brilliant physicists, but chemists and even biologists. It is recorded that one eminent Professor (J W S Pringle) was summoned to the Air Ministry for interview in connection with TRE. He had never heard of radar, but he bought a book

---

* 'radar' was a word unknown until 1943/44 when it was introduced into the English language by the United States. For security reasons up till 1943/44 radar was known as RDF (Radio Direct Finding) or Telecommunications in England.

on radio and read up on the subject in the train on his journey to London. A month later he appeared as a radar expert at Worth Matravers and became a prominent member of the team. The enthusiasm and application of gifted men was to contribute as much to TRE as specialised knowledge.

The view had been advanced that the best head of a research organisation must be a man of wide education but not a trained scientist. The scientific specialist tends to be biased in favour of his own projects and intolerant of lay opinion, and is moreover frequently handicapped by inability to present a case persuasively in writing. Some have held that the Royal Aircraft Establishment, Farnborough, would not have laid itself open to such frequent and violent criticism had it been free from scientific leadership. If this is true the Chief Superintendent of TRE, Dr A P Rowe, provided a brilliant exception to the rule. For this eminent scientist was far more than a scientist; he was also a man of very great administrative ability and wide vision, with a strong sense of the value of accessibility and personal contacts.

The outstanding success of TRE could only have been achieved with quite remarkable leadership. Men of genius (of whom there were a number at Swanage) do not fit easily into a team, nor are University professors naturally amenable to discipline; and scientists do not always work happily with those who have to apply their theories. There were about 1000 men and women – from boffins to bottle washers – employed at TRE (and the number increased to 3000 later). Rowe didn't worry if there was not unbroken harmony and unimpeachable discipline in his empire; he was satisfied if he could obtain – and he did obtain – complete dedication to the end in view (that is, winning the war) without any nonsense about self-interest, and complete understanding between the inventor and the Service which was to use the invention. He saw his task as making contact between 'the man with a need and the man with a technique.'

One method he employed to secure this contact was what

came to be known as 'Sunday Soviets.' These were meetings held on Sundays in Rowe's office at Worth Matravers, and later at Malvern, to which he invited Cabinet Ministers, senior officers of the RAF and the other Services, research scientists and operational pilots. Here questions of importance were thrashed out between the men who made the policy, the men who provided the tools and the men who did the job. This kind of meeting couldn't have happened in Germany – which is perhaps the reason why, in the use of radar, we were usually one step ahead of the enemy.

Practically all the new ideas about radar were born at Worth Matravers during the years 1940-41; the later years of the war were spent in developing them. When the war started only ground radar was in operation, with a range of some 60-80 miles, which enabled the approach of enemy bombers to be detected anywhere on the south and east coast. Airborne radar had not yet started. I arrived at Christchurch at the tail end of the Battle of Britain, when the night bombing of London had started and all the heat of research was turned on to Air Interception (AI) so that night fighters might be able to locate and destroy night bombers. Other objectives of radar research which were to have a decisive influence on the war, such as the detection of ships and submarines at sea, the location of target areas by night bombers and the pinpointing of special targets by Pathfinders, were still in their early stages.

The task of the Flying Unit was to co-operate with the scientists in experimental flights to test the results of their researches.

The presence of many civilians at Christchurch made it a most unusual station. The RAF found some of their new colleagues very strange in dress and manner, and at times mirth-provoking, but we had a great respect and admiration for them. In many flights the aircraft had, as passengers, scientists who had only enthusiasm to see them through the ordeals of an unfamiliar exercise; and pilots on the whole formed a high opinion of the boffin's performance as a part-time aviator.

My first passenger surprised me by wearing his helmet the wrong way round. I couldn't make out, at first, why his headgear looked so different for it resembled a Victorian poke bonnet. On sorting him out I learnt that he had never flown before and had received no instruction whatsoever regarding flight preparation, use of parachute etc. Yet he was mad keen to get airborne to see if his equipment would work. On his knees he held his so called 'breadboard', bearing a highly complex piece of radar equipment to be tested.

As the flight proceeded the colour drained from his face and eventually he was sick over his breadboard, which shortcircuited the whole concern and started a small fire. This was extinguished and we returned to base. I began to realise that I was flying for a very unusual organisation.

But not all the boffins were ignorant of flying. Some had already flown a fair amount in the attempt to get radar airborne.

Robert Watson-Watt who has some claim to be called the 'Father of Radar' (though like most great inventions radar was of very mixed parentage) was a frequent visitor to the unit. He would arrive from the Ministry in his London suiting and be stuffed into a flying suit, fitted with a parachute and helmet with oxygen mask and then waddle out to a Blenheim looking like a large benign teddy bear.

Our top priority at that time was to produce some form of airborne radar to enable our night fighters to find enemy bombers on their nightly incursions over England. And Robert Watson-Watt not only kept up the pressure but saw the end results himself.

Accompanied by a boffin eager to demonstrate his latest brainchild they would both clamber up onto the top of a Blenheim fuselage and force themselves down through the rear hatch into the incredibly narrow interior.

Off we would roar to some 18,000 feet to hunt for our

target; one of our own aircraft often hiding in cloud and usually heading in a North Westerly direction towards the Bristol Channel.

It was curious that we pilots developed such confidence in our boffins and their equipment that the thought of collision hardly occurred to us. Our 'hunting' usually ended in a tail chase with the boffin giving accurate distances from the unseen target but there were moments of anxiety such as hitting the 'wash' of an unseen target in cloud coinciding with the boffin remarking that he had lost the blip. It was a case of nose up, throttle back 20 degrees of flap and hope for the best! Such return to reality could be quiet exciting.

So great was the need for something, anything, to deal with the night bombing menace that a couple of successful trial flights would result in the aircraft and its equipment being delivered that same day along the coast to RAF Ford near Littlehampton for operational trials against the Luftwaffe that same night. If successful the unit's workshops could equip a whole squadron with handmade sets by the end of a week. Such was the urgency in the autumn of 1940.

It was exacting work but we were just ordinary mortals and this was as it should be. If the boffin produced an idea so complex that we couldn't handle it it was no good introducing it to the Service. Failures of equipment were frequent but the need for it was desperate. The technical advice given us to clear faults was usually within our educational capacity to understand and often consisted of some broad technical advice such as 'if it packs up give that box of carbon piles a kick. It may come to life again!'

After the highest priorities had been given to the night bombing menace priorities changed, were indeed always changing. This time it was for a navigational aid for Bomber Command.

A Dr Dippy had dreamed up a system of navigation which subsequently became known as 'Gee'. One of the great contributions to winning the war. The first trial flight in

Wellington N 2761 took place on the 17th May 1941 when with a boffin called Bellringer working the trial equipment we flew off from Christchurch to the North to see how far away we could receive the signals. We thought we might get as far as the Derby-Crewe area. With Bellringer in a mounting fever of excitement we ended up fifty miles East of Dundee before the signals weakened. At last we had a navigational aid that would cover a lot of Germany and the whole of England.

Calibration of radar ground stations was also one of the tasks of the unit. For this work we usually flew fighter aircraft singly from various points on the South Coast over the channel towards France. Only after the war did I discover that many of these flights were to calibrate not our own ground stations as we thought but the German radars known as Freyas!

For some strange reason the Germans radioed their plots by morse code to their defence headquarters; a code which was quickly broken and the signals could easily be heard in England. We were able to judge the Freya's efficiency by listening to their signals recording our own range etc. There was no danger in these trips. Our own radar was so superb that if a belligerent situation developed we would be warned and hightail it back home.

Although the Special Duty Flight was an experimental and not a combatant unit, we were operating on the fringe of hostilities and were always liable to get caught up in enemy action. We had a few Spitfires and Hurricanes, and when Southampton was raided we would take off in them to defend our own airfield. Our small 'incidents' were generally fought under favourable conditions, close to home base, full tanks and our own superb radar control. Such incidents we did experience were catching an enemy bomber limping back to France on one engine. Nothing very heroic but my Flight Commander, Douglas Rayment, accounted for $2\frac{1}{2}$ victims before becoming a victim himself.

28 August 1939. Refuelling at Mersa Matruh, Egypt. This took two hours! All fuel had to be filtered through washleathers. The fuel was in tin cans which were individually packed in wooden boxes. The procedure was to break open the wooden box, put an axe through the tin of petrol and hoist it up to the wing. The hardest job was to avoid getting splashed; and smoking was discouraged! The Germans had already invented the Jerrycan

En route from UK to Singapore. Mersa Matruh, 28 August 1939. Crew of Blenheim L 1104. *L to R:* The imperturbable Pidd, Fitter, the Author wearing regulation topee, Air Observer Sgt Willmott who shared the piloting (unofficially), and Aircraftsman Templeton, Wireless Operator and sole external navigational aid

The relaxed LAC Pidd looks on while Sergeant Willmott flies Blenheim L 1104 over Rutbah Wells, Iraq, at 12,000 feet, end of August 1939

Sheik's Levees guarding Blenheim L 1104 at Sharjah, 2 September 1939, the day before war broke out

Flying Officer Harley Boxall on his return to RAF Tengah, Singapore, after being marooned on the uninhabited island of Ko Rawi. Suspended from his right hand is the dinghy sea anchor which he wore as a hat during his Robinson Crusoe existence.

Dec. 1940. The Author familiarising himself with the various switches and controls of the newly delivered United States DB7 (afterwards known as the Boston). So superior was the performance of this bomber that it was adapted as a night fighter after being fitted with guns and Air Interception Radar.
Photo: Douglas Fisher

On 14th January 1941, I was flying a Hurricane to carry out an experimental interception against a 'friendly,' under the instructions of a ground controller at Worth Matravers. My instructions were to climb to 10,000 feet over Worth Matravers and await further orders. My call sign was 'Blood Orange.' Presently the ground control operator came through on the R/T in a strong Liverpool accent.

'Blood Orange, Blood Orange. We have some bandits for you about 30 miles south approaching you at angels ten (10,000 feet).'

My mouth went dry. How many 'bandits' were there? I was in a good position, nearly over England, and had the great advantage of GCI (Ground Control Interception) to tell me what the enemy were doing. I decided to gain some height and while waiting for further news to prepare for my new role by brushing up my aerobatics. So I climbed to 13,000 feet and started a loop. As I was about to pull out of my dive there was a crack and a terrific jerk, and I found the stick solid in my hand and impossible to move.

The Hurricane went on down. I thought the enemy must have been closer than reported and that I had been shot down. When I saw the panels covering the ammunition boxes on the wings come off – which only happened when 300 mph was exceeded – I knew that things were pretty desperate. So I decided to bale out.

Then I made a bad mistake. I undid my straps first and tried to open the cockpit canopy next. It wouldn't open, and I realised I should have dealt with the canopy before undoing my straps. I was still heading straight down, and there couldn't be many seconds to go. I heard the swish of the Great Reaper's scythe.

In thrashing about with my legs while I struggled with the canopy I must have knocked the stick forward. At some fantastic speed the aircraft started to do a 'bunt', that is a reverse loop, with my head on the outside of the circle – an unusual and strictly prohibited manoeuvre. I was thrown into the canopy with a force 8 or 9 times that of gravity, remaining conscious and able to see as I came round with that tremendous pressure. When upside down I was at cloud level, 2,000 feet. The aircraft had come down 11,000 feet in its dive.

I had pain in my eyes and head, but I could still see. Although lodged in the roof I was able to reach down and get hold of the spade grip at the top of the stick. Instinctively (Sergeant Forster's training in 'recovery from unusual positions' at Grantham Flying Training School still lingered in my sub-conscious), I pushed the stick to one side, and the aircraft rolled out and came upright. I fell from the roof into my seat. Instinctively again I opened the throttle; the engine responded and, with tremendous vibration the aircraft flew level just below the cloud base.

I found my sight far from normal; I could distinguish sea from land and sky from cloud, but all definition had been lost. Guided by the sun I flew north towards where I thought Christchurch would be. Then that Liverpool voice called again:

'Hullo Blude Orege. Hullo Blude Orege. We cannot see you, Blude Orege. What is your position?'

I could only reply that I had 'had an incident' and was returning to base.

The coast came into view, with Christchurch harbour, as I thought, on my left. I flew towards what I imagined was the airfield, but as I approached decided it must be Poole park. I opened the throttle and the aircraft flew on with fearful vibration. As I juddered round Poole harbour I identified a blob in the middle as Brownsea Island and knew exactly where I was. Checking by Bournemouth's two piers I came down in Christchurch airfield, overrunning the landing area and ending up against the barbed wire. I switched off and just sat.

My eyes were protruding from my head and wildly bloodshot, and my face was weirdly discoloured (within twelve hours I was black from the chest upwards). I was taken straight to Boscombe Hospital, and doctors from the Royal Aircraft Establishment, Farnborough, came to see me next day. They named my trouble *petechial haemorrhage*, caused by the force of 8 or 9 'G' to which I had been subjected at the bottom of the bunt. Other Hurricane pilots had been found dead with the same symptoms. I was the first to have got away with it.

The cause of the trouble was that the heavy 'G' loading at the bottom of the loop had burst a large bottom panel of fabric backed with ply, letting air under pressure into the rear of the fuselage; this had stripped off the fabric from the rear part of the fuselage and it had become wrapped round the elevators. An order appeared shortly afterwards that Hurricanes would not be dived at more than 280 knots, and the offending panel was strengthened.

I was kept in the dark at Boscombe and was fit for flying again in a week. So was the Hurricane.

Christchurch had an unusual excitement on 5th May 1941. The air raid warning sounded and pilots leapt into the fighters and waited for instructions from Worth Matravers, which had the radar picture of what was going on. I was in a Spitfire waiting for orders to start when I was amazed to see a small biplane with full German markings come flying in over Christchurch harbour and touch down on the airfield in front of me. Was this the start of the invasion? If so, why had there been no shooting? The plane had landed straight over the top of an AA post which hadn't fired a shot. What on earth was going on? Then a swarm of 24 RAF fighter aircraft flew overhead, obviously to deal with the invader.

One of the airfield defence soldiers advanced stolidly on the intruder with fixed bayonet and rifle at the ready. A man in the rear cockpit raised both his hands ... The invasion had surrendered.

Out of the plane came two young Frenchmen, who had

brought off one of the most remarkable exploits of the war. They had managed to get a job in the German aerodrome at Caen. One of them had been learning to fly, and had flown solo, but it must have been at least a year earlier, before the fall of France. They had seen a small German aircraft – a Bucker Jungmeister rather like a Tiger Moth – arrive. It was pushed into a hangar for the night, and was left near to the entrance. The two went in, examined the controls and worked out how the aircraft should be started; as they wore blue overalls, they doubtless looked fairly official. Next morning the Bucker was pushed out onto the tarmac. Carrying brooms the two Frenchmen went out to have another look at it; the trainee pilot got into the cockpit, the other swung the prop and jumped in behind, and in a few seconds they were airborne and heading across the Channel. They made a landfall at Bournemouth, turned right along the coast, and landed in the first likely-looking field they saw, not knowing it was an aerodrome – an unexpected tribute, incidentally, to the rudimentary camouflage at Christchurch, obtained mostly by dispersing the aircraft under trees.

Questioned about what they meant to do if attacked by fighters, they said they had brought a piece of white cloth with them to wave in the air! Never surely has fortune so favoured the brave as when these two young men trundled unmolested through the entire defence of the English coast.

The two adventurers were taken to London for interrogation leaving the Bucker with us. We repainted it, replacing crosses and swastikas with RAF roundels and for a whole day took turns to fly it. It was a delightful aircraft and a beauty for aerobatics. Then came an order from Air Ministry to send it to London, where it was to be put on show. So we had to paint back the crosses and swastikas and send it away by road.

Two outstanding pilots at Christchurch were the CO, Wing Commander Horner ('Jackie', as he was inevitably called), and my Flight Commander, Flight Lieutenant Douglas Rayment. Horner was the most polished performer on the station, whose aerobatics with their elegance and precision marked him as a real perfectionist. The Blenheim, though primarily a bomber, was equipped with four guns and often had to do duty as a fighter. When, with this in mind, I tried to do a slowroll I broke all the perspex in the rear turret. Rayment, hearing of this, took me in the passenger seat which only had a lap strap and showed me how to barrel roll a Blenheim with such smoothness and precision that I never left my seat! Compared with Douglas Rayment my flying was 'ham.'

One of the episodes on the fringe of hostilities occurred when I was the target aircraft on an air interception test and came out of cloud to find a Heinkel III in front of me. Douglas Rayment was in the intercepting aircraft. With a tallyho we both gave chase. The Heinkel dived into a patch of low stratus cloud over the Needles and Douglas followed him down. I kept above the cloud in case the enemy came back out on top. As there was no sign of the Heinkel when I arrived at the southern extremity of the low cloud, I dropped below and found Rayment circling round some wreckage. When we landed Douglas congratulated me on shooting the German down! Neither of us in fact had seen the Heinkel again or fired our guns! The Heinkel must have been in such a hurry to get home that it dived straight through the very low cloud into the sea.

But Douglas Rayment was one of my many friends who was lost in the war – the only fatal casualty at Christchurch. In July 1941, he was doing calibrations over the Channel, which was always thought to be a fairly safe job because the Worth Matravers radar station was there to warn of threatened attacks. He saw an aircraft on the sea and called up to say he was going down to investigate. Then he reported that it was a German flying boat marked with red crosses. And that was the last that was ever heard of Flight Lieutenant Douglas L. Rayment.

A small airfield like Christchurch might be expected to produce accidents, but in fact during my stay there only two occurred, neither of them serious. One of them was unfortunately caused by me. I was over the Bristol Channel in a Beaufort with a scientist called Reid, doing runs on lightships to calibrate some equipment used in attacking surface vessels. For this task the Beaufort carried large aerials under the wings rather like antlers and ten feet long. One of the two Taurus engines failed, and we set course for home. For a one-engined landing I would have been wiser to go to a larger airfield than Christchurch, but the fact remains that I didn't. I made a responsible approach but came in rather low, so that unknown to me one of the aerials picked up a spiral coil of the barbed wire surrounding the airfield and we ran on dragging several hundred yards of wire behind us. Then the Beaufort turned abruptly to port, my port wing tip bashed in the nose of a parked Wellington. This spun us round and we parked ourselves, still completely out of control, neatly in line with other aircraft dispersed under the trees. It was such an orderly arrival that no-one noticed the accident. Pausing only to pick some mushrooms growing under the wing Reid and I walked over to the flight office. Jackie Horner was not pleased nor was TRE. Not so much because of the damage to the Beaufort, the outstanding calibrations required had been obtained successfully on this, its last calibration flight, but the Wellington was about to start a flying programme with newly installed experimental navigational aids and their introduction to the service was delayed due to my being over-confident and not making my one engined landing at a bigger airfield. This is what the Air Officer Commanding said and he was right.

August 29th 1941 was a rather special day for me and for two boffins, Bedford and Downing, for they were to demonstrate the first use of 10 centimetre interception equipment to Robert Watson-Watt. The days of external aerials were past, instead, in an elongated nose covered by a plastic dome, was a large oscillating metal dish called a scanner which not only gave a picture of the aircraft to be intercepted but also a somewhat distorted but recognisable map of the ground beneath. It was especially good over the sea where the coastal indentations and islands could be clearly seen on the screen. We took off from Christchurch, climbed and headed south. Then we carried out a few interceptions on one of our own aircraft acting as 'target'. Finally German occupied Alderney and the Channel Islands appeared ahead of me. The boffins in the back had had them in sight for sometime but oblivious to danger as all boffins were when concentrating on their work, they chattered away in the excitment of the picture they saw.

I turned away and headed North. There was no reason to risk not only the equipment but the lives of the 'Father of Radar' and the boffins. Besides in less then 24 hours I had to be in the church at Highcliffe to be married in what was to be a typical wartime wedding. Married Saturday, honeymoon Sunday and back at work again on Monday.

Flying aircraft at SDF was pure joy.

RAF aircraft in the 1940's were still fairly unsophisticated and while types differed in many aspects such as fuel systems switches, undercarriage and flap levers, at least they all had one thing in common – the RAF standard flying intrument panel. Whoever had the bright idea of standardising the positions of the flying instruments deserves a medal. He must have saved hundreds of lives and many many training hours.

We, pilots of SDF, came to appreciate this standard-isation when we had to fly so many types without any dual. A study of the pilots' notes, a chat with the pilot who flew the aircraft in, if you were lucky, and off you went on your own. Of course aircraft were a lot cheaper then! Yet I cannot remember a single occasion of an incident during '1st solo on type'.

The groundcrews under Flight Sergeant Pritchard had an

even harder task discovering how to service the aircraft at all hours of day and night besides coping with modifications essential to the boffins' experiments. I suspect many of the airmen were hand-picked for we had an unusual number of Halton 'brats'; the service slang for any airman or officer who had been through the full regime at RAF Halton, 'The best public school in the UK'.

Of the 50 odd British and American types I flew at the unit my favourite was the Gladiator. The last and most advanced of the biplane fighters three of which, Faith, Hope and Charity were to gain immortal fame at Malta.

The Gladiator was used for testing ground radar. Being fabric covered it gave a poor radar response so it was a good test of ground equipment if it could detect a Gladiator at a fair distance.

On 1st November 1941 I was asked to fly a calibration flight in Gladiator K 8049 at 18,000 feet starting from Worth Matravers and flying in a southerly direction. I'm not sure whether it was to calibrate German radar reaction or to calibrate our own.

The flight was mainly in cloud and I wasn't the least concerned about being intercepted by the enemy because Worth Matravers could give me plenty of warning of enemy aircraft activity.

After twenty minutes I began to feel anxious. The cloud was breaking up. Perhaps they had lost my blip. Maybe I'd better give them a call on the vhf. Before I could transmit a large black puff appeared ahead of me to port and immediately afterwards another one to starboard. Then there was a tremendous explosion and I found myself upside down. I rolled out and dived under the cloud and there below me was Guernsey with its greenhouses glinting in the slanting sunlight.

This was my first experience of heavy flak: I've often wondered whether the concussive effect was so amazingly strong because I was in such a light aircraft, for near misses later on in four engined bombers never seemed so shattering.

It was easy to dive away and hare back to Christchurch where we found holes in the mainplanes and tailplane but no other damage. My only satisfaction out of this incident was the thought that I was possibly the only pilot to invade Fortress Europe in a biplane fighter departing from England after Dunkirk! It certainly made me appreciate what my 1914/19 predecessors experienced in biplanes with 'archie'. The Germans must have wondered what a lone biplane was doing over Guernsey. I never did discover why the boffins required the flight. One didn't ask.

Life at SDF Christchurch was hectic, totally absorbing and marvellously interesting.

During the years of 1940 and 1941 our boffins were at their most productive. We ignorant pilots did not understand the working of their devices nor did we wish to learn too much in case we were ever captured and interrogated but we did experience their end products and marvelled at their achievements.

A stranger visiting Christchurch or Worth Matravers would have thought that the organisation was a self adjusting shambles. And so it was but it achieved remarkable results through lack of rigid control. Strange men would appear, cut holes in aeroplanes and stick odd looking aerials on them or cut off the nose of an aircraft to install such things as a large saucer shaped scanner. Whether they were safe to fly after such butchery was the responsibility of an aerodynamicist. Luckily he was never wrong. Meanwhile this heterogeneous collection of aircraft were prepared for flight by Flight Sergeant Pritchard and his team of 'erks'.

During this splendid period such famous devices as Gee (Navigational Aid), Rebecca/Eureka (Homing Device), H_2S (10 centimetre airborne radar which gave a visual presentation of the ground features through cloud or darkness), Oboe (very high level and extremely accurate blind bombing device), ASV (surface vessel location) and other war winners were born and brought to an operational state. The achievements were breathtaking. In the later years despite the enormous increase in size of the organisation the fruits were smaller.

We flew whenever the weather was fit and often when it was unfit for we had magnificent ground equipment at Worth Matravers and Sopley, an experimental GCI station, to control us. In weather which was so bad that normally we should have diverted to land elsewhere, they would offer to talk us down 'to have a look' so we would follow their directions until we would hear 'It's all yours now – the airfield should be in front of you.' We knew every ground feature on the approaches for we virtually only had the choice of two directions to land in bad conditions, East or West and it was easy to memorise them.

By October 1941 the unit had grown so large that Christchurch could no longer contain it. At the same time the new airfield at Hurn only 5 miles away was approaching completion so off we went to Hurn and just in time for four engined aircraft were now the playthings of the boffins. A separate naval section was formed under command of a naval officer to cater especially for naval research requirements and this enabled me to fulfil a longfelt desire to do some flying boat handling.

CHAPTER 6

Water, Wrens and Walruses

The Walrus looked as though she should be waterborne. She sat on the tarmac like a broody duck with her tail down on the floor. Incongruous in her design she had a boat's bow in which you could stand up, throw out an anchor, tend moorings or, if you felt inclined, you could mount the gun and shoot at your enemies in a 100 mile an hour gale. Behind the bow compartment there was a cockpit with room for two to sit side by side, the pilot being on the left. It was strange that the throttle and mixture controls were the same as a Spitfire's but both aircraft came from the same 'stable', 'Supermarine'. Further aft, under the wings, there was a wireless compartment and further aft still another hatch which, when removed, enabled you to mount a gun for defence purposes or embark and disembark from a dinghy, though the more usual method was via the pilot's cockpit. Standing in the after hatch the mighty Pegasus radial engine was above your head and slightly forward but it 'blew backwards' for it was mounted between the biplane wings. Under the outer end of each lower mainplane was a float. The whole of this bizarre and archaic looking contraption was held together by a mass of bracing wires and it all worked. In fact, as I was to discover, it was possibly the best flying boat ever built for getting airborne in rough seas for the single engine was reasonably protected from spray as it was a pusher with the propeller and ignition behind the wings. Other and much larger flying boats with their engines in front of the wings would throw water up on to their two inner engines from their bowwave. The electrics didn't like this.

The Walrus was a true amphibian for it had wheels, which retracted neatly into the side of the hull, so that you could land on land or land on water. The wheels could also be lowered when taxiing on the water. This effectively reduced the taxiing speed; a great advantage when manoeuvring. An unusual feature was a klaxon horn which blew in your ear whenever you throttled back whether the wheels were up or down. It was so easy to forget the wheels when landing on land or have them down when landing on water, which could be just as embarrassing. Either way it could be expensive and as the aeroplane didn't know land from water it had to rely on the pilot deciding whether to have the wheels up or down for a landing. The horn therefore always blew when you throttled back to go into land and this made you look at the surface you had chosen to land on and then at the wheels to check where they were. You could then trip out the horn but this would reactivate itself if you opened the throttle again, if only slightly. A dicey landing at sea trying to choose a calm patch by just keeping her airborne with power surges inevitably meant landing with the horn screaming in your ear but it was all good fun when you knew how. As yet I didn't know how but I was very keen to learn.

The newly formed naval section at Hurn was commanded by a very 'press-on' naval lieutenant called Stanley Adams. I asked him whether it would be possible to do some water landings and take-offs in the Walrus.

'How about after lunch?' came the reply. 'I want to check those new yagi aerials (referring to the 'toast racks' sticking out from each wing). They work all right and stand up to airfield landings but I should check that they will stand up to a bashing from the sea.'

Two o'clock on this April afternoon found me riding my bicycle with my parachute over my shoulder round the perimeter track en route to the Walrus for my initiation. I couldn't help but notice that the Windsock had its tail in the air. 'Isn't there too much wind?' I asked Stanley. 'It'll be a bit rough but that's what we are looking for' he replied.

I sat in the seat alongside him. We clattered into the air and I pumped up the wheels. The coast appeared and I noticed a few white horses on the water. We flew over Bournemouth and then low over the water for a couple of miles heading South South West into the eye of the wind.

I hadn't strapped myself in. It was in the days before the 'Strap yourself in' and 'Fly with Prudence' campaign had started.

The waves rolled by underneath, much bigger now when we were low down. I was beginning to wish that I hadn't come.

I never knew for certain whether Stanley meant to land when he did or whether the decision was taken by the Walrus. He had got as far as saying 'You must keep the Air Speed Indicator at 48 knots and wait for a calm pa...' when the thing happened. I regained awareness to find that I was curled up in the bow bleeding from small abrasions. The waves breaking on the hull assured me that I was still alive and that we were still afloat. I disentangled myself from the stowed front gun and scrambled back to my seat. I was not impressed with Stanley's idea of a calm patch.

Stanley was quite unperturbed by the landing, which he seemed to think was fairly normal. He lowered the wheels to reduce taxiing speed, for with the wheels up the waves broke freely over the windscreen and flowed down the cockpit hatch. Meanwhile Stanley was giving Part Two of his lecture. 'How to take off in the open sea'.

'She weathercocks naturally you see but rather than take off dead into wind I like to get the wind on the port bow to take up the swing as you open the throttle. Then I look at the sun, if there is one, to keep her straight during take-off; there will be so much water coming over the windscreen that it would be hopeless trying to watch the sea itself. I'd do up your straps,' he concluded. I did them up, very thoroughly. I could see fields and farms over the starboard wingtip and thought how nice it must be just to work on a farm.

I pumped up the wheels, Stanley gave her a burst and some right rudder which put the wind on the port bow. He then opened up fully. It was soon plain why it was useful to look at the sun. There seemed to be water everywhere. It poured through the innumerable cracks in the side windows and the hatch, and it felt as if the whole aircraft was about to disintegrate with the bashing and pounding.

I was not quite sure what happened next, but I think we became airborne and then stalled, with the port wingtip hitting the water first. The straps saved me from further injury, but the Walrus lay over at a drunken angle with the port wingtip in the water. We could then see that the wing float was loose and had been bent up sideways under the wing. It was still in a position to give us some buoyancy but the angle at which we lay was disturbing.

'Get out on the starboard wing' yelled Stanley. I scrambled out of the cockpit and worked my way along the wing until she righted herself. There were plenty of struts and rigging wires to hang on to. The engine, to my surprise, was still running and this gave us our usual fast taxiing speed; much too fast, for the bow, as it crashed into the waves, was throwing water everywhere. Then Stanley lowered the wheels, and with the reduced speed everything became comparatively calm.

Standing in the cockpit, like a parson in his pulpit, Stanley shouted his views on the situation. 'It's too rough to take off out here. I'll taxi over to Swanage Bay where it should be calmer.'

The prospect was far from engaging; we were about five miles from Swanage Bay, and even if we ever got there I didn't fancy trying to take off with only one float serviceable. However Stanley was Captain of the ship so off we set for Swanage Bay.

At the start Stanley taxied with the wheels down but soon he raised them. With the much higher taxiing speed I suffered considerably for I was frequently covered by spray. Fortunately we were moving across wind so that my position on the lee side was comparatively protected by the hull from the full force of the waves. My weight kept the leeside float in the water and this drag stopped her from weathercocking into the wind.

After about a quarter of an hour Stanley throttled back, lowered the wheels and stood up in the cockpit to ask how I was getting on. I said that I was all right but had my doubts about taking off in Swanage Bay; I suggested taxiing into Poole Harbour, where there was a Walrus Unit and a slip for us to taxi onto.

Stanley received this suggestion with horror. 'But it's a naval unit isn't it?'. 'Yes' I replied. 'Anyway it would mean taxiing downwind and we'd have to get the drogues out to do that,' he shouted.

Whereat he lowered himself into the cockpit muttering something about washing dirty linen on your own doorstep. We set off again for Swanage Bay. Another quarter of an hour passed, and by that time I was beginning to feel cold and numb. I had had enough of flying boats.

But Stanley was right about Swanage Bay; the sea was much calmer as we taxied into it. He lowered the wheels, stood up in his cockpit and said that he would let her weathercock while he went down aft and pumped out the bilges.

The Walrus taxied slowly upwind while I still stood up on the wing in my misery. On the headland in front of me was the hotel where, only a few months before, I had spent my 24 hour honeymoon; and here I was wet, wretched and frightened wearing the very same uniform in which I had been married! The thought of the imminent take-off worried me. The bay didn't seem very large, and it looked doubtful whether, even if we got off the water, we would be able to climb over Durlston Head, which was the headland sheltering us from the wind.

Before long I noticed that we were getting very close to the shore, but with the noise of the engine it was useless to shout to Stanley as he pumped the bilges inside the hull down aft. So the Walrus sogged gently in the waves and gradually edged towards the beach. When Stanley at last appeared the fact that we were nearly ashore didn't worry him in the least. He got into his seat and taxied downwind towards the Old Harry rocks.

The moment of truth had come. We swung into the wind then Stanley popped up for another conference. This time there were to be no mistakes. The craft was pumped dry and the sea was reasonably calm but we still had to keep the starboard wing down until enough aileron control was obtained to balance the aircraft. As soon as he raised the wheels our forward speed, coupled with the strong headwind, gave him full control and I dived into the cockpit and slammed the hatch shut. To my surprise we got off perfectly smoothly without any preliminary banging and crashing. We rose high over Durlston Head and set course for Hurn. As we flew over Bournemouth I noticed that the port float was still there held by its rigging wires in a stable position under the wing. I just hoped that it wouldn't fall on any of the good citizens beneath us.

Next morning I was driving round the dispersals with the Station Commander. As we passed the Walrus some naval ratings were working on it re-rigging the wingtip float. The Station Commander remarked that we must do something about getting the airfield fenced in. He'd heard that some forest ponies had been in to the airfield during the night and had damaged the Walrus's wingtip float rubbing their backs against it.

It was a strange lapse on the part of the German High Command that Worth Matravers and Swanage were left unbombed during the years 1940 and 1941. But by the spring of 1942 the Air Ministry had reason to think that the lapse would soon be rectified especially after our Bruneval raid, so plans were set on foot to remove TRE to a safer place. Here a difficulty was encountered: high grade civilian scientists are not so easy to move as military units, and our boffins were perfectly happy where they were. They liked the situation and found it admirably suited to their work, and were much too busy to contemplate the disturbance and commotion which would be caused by a move.

Whether, as was authoritatively stated, twenty-seven train loads of German paratroops were in fact assembled in France ready to attack TRE is open to doubt; what is not in doubt is that a battalion of infantry arrived to defend the Establishment; proceeded to entangle the place in barbed wire and generally made life so impossible that a move to a more more peaceful location began to take on the aspect of a blessed release. This was perhaps the first successful application by a Government department of a Hitlerite technique – the war of nerves!

The place selected as the new home of TRE was Malvern College. This unlucky school, which had already been evacuated once during the war and then restored to its own premises, was now turned out for the second time. The migration took place on 25th May 1942. At the same time we flew our aircraft up to RAF Defford, a hastily constructed airfield about twelve miles from Malvern. It was large enough to hold eventually over 100 aircraft and was commanded by a Group Captain. I flew a Hudson up to the new station and took with me our half-dozen hens. It is an interesting fact, not generally known to poultry farmers, that reduced atmospheric pressure makes hens lay in the air. Mine were no exception.

A week after the move Swanage was heavily bombed.

On our move from the South Coast to RAF Defford the Naval Unit expanded considerably for Naval requirements were increasing rapidly.

To ease the workload on the scientists Wrens were posted in to carry out routine calibration work and testing of trial equipment in the air. They were all young, mainly in their teens and early twenties, and they all had two things in common, high intelligence and an ability to absorb the intricacies of radar rapidly.

While we had been stationed at Christchurch and Hurn we had carried out our airborne calibration work over the English Channel and the Bristol Channel and we had occasionally been embarrassed by enemy activity.

Now that we were further north we started to use the Irish Sea, mainly in the Liverpool Bay area, and being further away from the enemy we were undoubtedly lulled into a false sense of security.

July 28th 1942 was a gorgeous summer's day and to help out the Naval Section I offered to fly a detail in a Swordfish P4008 with two Wrens, Palmer and Jackson. We were to do some calibration runs with experimental equipment on our standard target, the Bar Lightship, some 20 miles out in the Irish Sea from Liverpool.

We flew over Llangollen, the Horseshoe Pass, down the Vale of Clwyd, and in rather hazy conditions over Prestatyn and out to sea. It didn't take the girls long to pick up the Bar Lightship and in half an hour we had completed our work.

I was just turning for home when one of the girls said that she had a mass of ships on the tube about twenty miles away. I thought it would be educational for them to see a convoy en route so I let them home me on to the ships.

Normally I wouldn't have dreamt of flying near a convoy. Past experience in RAF monoplanes and especially Blenheims which were so like Junkers 88's had taught me that mariners were inclined to be trigger happy and would shoot first and identify the aircraft afterwards.

But I felt safe in a Swordfish. Being a biplane and well known to most sailors it was easily identified and respected. Anyway I didn't intend to go too near the convoy, just near enough to show the girls that their equipment really worked and let them appreciate what a magnificent sight it was to see a big convoy underway.

We flew on at 2000 feet and soon the convoy came in sight ahead of us with its balloons flying above. I told the girls to stop directing and to stick their heads out and have a look.

Almost at the same time the peace of this summer's day was broken. Black puffs appeared over the whole length of the convoy; they looked all the world like the musical notation of one of Chopin's mazurkas. Then out of this hail of anti-aircraft fire came a Junkers 88 hightailing towards Holyhead at sea level. He was at least three times faster than we were and it was no part of my job to get mixed up in a dangerous military situation in an old biplane with two girls aboard, so I turned away heading in the direction of the Welsh coast.

Thinking that there might possibly be other enemy aircraft around I cocked the front gun and fired a few rounds just to make sure that it was working. It was the only armament we carried; was of the 1914-18 war vintage in design and was mounted by the pilot's right knee whence it fired miraculously through the propeller being so timed by its Constantinescu gear that, hopefully, the bullets were projected between the propeller blades and not through them.

Almost immediately after firing smoke filled the front cockpit and on sticking my head over the starboard side I was disturbed to see flames along the side of the fuselage issuing from the gun position.

My mouth went dry. The petrol tank was just above and to one side of the burning gun, the sea was by now deserted and not a ship was in sight and I had two Wrens in the back as yet

71

unaware of the conflagration in front.

Having read lots of 1914-18 war literature I dived steeply down to sea level in an attempt to blow out the flames. The stringbag* screamed down attaining at least 150 knots and the smoke and flame died.

In the prevailing haze it was difficult to know how far away from land we were but in due course and to my great relief the heartening sight of Rhyl's magnificent beach came in sight. A natural landing ground should we need it.

Having arrived over land morale returned. The aircraft flew normally and having circled Rhyl a couple of times without any further pyrotechnic phenomenon manifesting itself I set course for the Horseshoe Pass and RAF Defford.

On landing the cause of the fire was only too apparent and entirely my own fault. I had failed to remove the oily gun cover prior to take off! The incendiaries had set it on fire. Admittedly, to save cleaning guns, we normally left the gun covers on for local flying. There is a moral in this story somewhere. However Wrens Palmer and Jackson could truly say that they had flown in operational conditions and had an experience outside the run of normal research duties.

We also enjoyed episodes at Defford not to be looked for in the work of a fighting service in wartime. Such a day was the 5th August 1942 when with 'Joe' Sellick as co-pilot and Wrens Palmer and Sharp as radar operators we set off to do a fairly long programme of work in the Cardigan Bay area.

We had taken the unexpired portion of the day's rations with us with the intention of eating while airborne and completing what, in effect, was two sorties in only one flight. It had been a long tiring morning and by noon we were hot, tired and wilting with the roar of the Mercury engine of our Sea Otter 8854. The lovely weather, the calm sea and St

---

* stringbag: Service parlance for Swordfish so named because the large number of interplane flying wires made it look like a stringbag!

Tudwals Islands and Abersoch beach looked so inviting that we dropped down, landed in the bay and threw out our anchor while we had lunch in blessed silence sunbathing on top of the fuselage and the lower mainplanes.

What bliss it was to fly an amphibian which could land in such lovely places as Abersoch Bay. No wonder it is called the Naples of the North, this pearl of the Lleyn peninsula, and how lucky we were to be personnel of an experimental unit which could enjoy such liberties.

Our euphoria would have been shortlived had we but known that 13 days later Joe Sellick was to die with his navigator brother in an Anson aircraft on a delivery flight when the inadequately glued plywood covering the leading edge of the port wing broke away 'like a pack of cards,' as a witness stated, and they spun in to their deaths near Cirencester.

So died Flight Lieutenant E T Sellick DFC already one of the few survivors of a Beaufort squadron of 'shipbusters' specialising in attacking German convoys off the Norwegian coast.

He had been posted to TFU for a rest period from operational flying only to find that the Reaper was waiting for him and he met his death all because of an inadequately mixed pot of glue.

On another occasion (18 November 1942) with Stanley Adams and photographer Douglas Fisher we were flying home across the Irish Sea in Walrus L2201 when I saw a Lancashire nobby trawling in the channel near the Point of Ayr Lighthouse in the Dee Estuary. I knew the area well for I had worked on the fishing nobbies during the depression. It was low tide and so the sandbanks were up and the sea in the channels was calm. I realised conditions were ideal for a water landing and it might be possible to get some fish.

The nobby had just hauled his trawl and was heading back uptide and upwind to make another trawl over the same ground. Conditions couldn't be better. If we could taxi up behind him and get him to tow us it would keep us apart (and save damage to our lightly clad hull) and we should be able to get some fish.

I handed over to Stanley Adams who was our ace Walrus water handler. After landing I took the bow position as we taxied up behind the nobby. I recognised the skipper as Sam Roberts of Bagillt and gave him the signal to keep steaming and take a line. (You don't throw ropes at flying boats because it is so embarrassing if the rope goes into a whirring propeller). Luckily the Lancashire nobby has a very low freeboard so that the crew can get their trawls aboard easily. Stanley lowered the Walrus wheels and held her with superb judgement just two feet away from the nobby's stern. I threw the rope to Sam Roberts who made fast, and Stanley throttled back to tick-over speed which was slow enough with our wheels down for the nobby to tow us.

Sam Roberts handed me three bucketfuls of fish which I had to pour out into the bilges as we hadn't anything to put them in. I put two halfcrowns in the last bucket as I handed it back and he cast us off.

We were soon airborne and landed back at Defford an hour later with the dying fish still flapping in the bilges.

22 years later I found where Sam Roberts lived in Bagillt. He told me that as he was the only boat out that day he and his boy crew had difficulty in persuading their friends that an aeroplane had actually landed by them and bought some fish. Luckily I was still in touch with Douglas Fisher our photographer who had taken photographs of this piscatorial operation. He sent me a set of photographs which I presented to Sam Roberts, which he proudly displayed on his mantelpiece.

One of the simpler and most useful devices which the boffins invented was called Walter. It consisted of a small telescopic mast and a very small amount of boffinery powered by a tiny battery. This was packed into the pilots parachute seat pack. When he landed in the sea, desert or jungle he merely extended the mast and held it up. The clever part of the device was that it didn't use power or switch itself on unless an aircraft searching with a powerful radar equipment (eg Rebecca) activated it. The aircraft was then able to read not only its distance from the Walter but also to home on to it. But first we had to make it work.

We were very conscious that all equipment had to be tested operationally however well it performed on basic trials. Our Wing Commander 'Jackie' Horner decided that he'd better jump out into the Irish Sea and then see if anyone could find him. He realised that the sooner it could be proved and introduced to the services the more lives could be saved by the device.

As we didn't want to lose him I arranged for the Marine Craft Unit at Pwllheli to send a launch some 8 miles south of Bardsey Island. We then briefed a couple of aircraft carrying Rebecca equipment 'to search Cardigan Bay and find a ditched pilot.'

I flew Jackie Horner over to Cardigan Bay in a Wellington. Not an ideal aircraft to jump out of as its exits, to preserve the strength of the geodetics, were very small. He decided that he would drop out of the trap under the pilot's compartment backwards. I advised him to have hold of the ripcord 'D' ring before he left the aircraft and to hang on to it when he pulled it so that we could keep the inventory straight.

Came the moment of truth at 2400 feet and having made certain the marine craft section had positioned their launch Jackie dropped out. After surfacing, he got rid of his chute, inflated his dinghy, climbed in and erected his telescopic mast. He received a series of small electric shocks and none of the searching aircraft found him! So much for doing an operational trial. The impact on landing had broken one of the contacts. It was as well that we had asked the Marine Craft Unit to stand by.

After modifications to the equipment the Scientist responsible for its design offered to test it himself. He was a large man, was Banner, but a splendid 'press-on' type and there was a certain amount of doubt as to whether he was too large to launch himself through the hatch in the floor particularly when he was equipped with his flying clothing, parachute and dinghy. However gravity was on his side and away he went. The parachute opened, the dinghy inflated, he clambered aboard and erected his Walter aerial without, this time, any shocks. The search aircraft found him immediately. He had proved his own equipment and within a matter of days it was available to service pilots to carry packed in their dinghies which in turn formed the seat of their parachute pack.

What very brave men Jackie Horner and Banner were. Neither had jumped out of an aeroplane before, yet to prove a life saving device quickly, on a cold October day they had launched themselves out of an aeroplane without any reserve parachute to land in a rough Irish Sea.

And all this was done without reference to higher authority. Such was the latitude allowed to the TFU. The operational trials were completed in a matter of days under the spur of war. In peacetime it would have taken months merely to get the permission to jump in the sea.

Since then Walter and similar homing devices using the same principle have saved numerous aircrew at sea and not only at sea for the device can of course be used on land. One pilot is known to have hung for many hours in a tree in the Burmese forest until being finally located by the Rebecca/ Walter system.

The 20th November, 1942, dawned with a strong unstable north-westerly airstream and the promise of bad weather to come.

I was sitting in my flight office mid-morning, grateful for a quiet spell to get on with some paperwork, when the 'phone rang.

It was Lieutenant Stanley Adams of the Naval Section. 'Griff,' he said, 'there's an urgent need to get the Walrus and its new installation up to Arbroath today. I'm shorthanded. Could you fly it for me?' I hesitated. Then he added, 'I can let you have Wren Palmer as crew. She has to go up anyway to work the installation.'

I loved flying the Walrus but the Royal Naval Air Station at Arbroath near Dundee was an awful long way away from Defford, and with this northerly airstream it would be a long haul. But it was an interesting challenge and I accepted.

A quick visit to the Met Office merely confirmed my fears that a 25 to 30 knot headwind was predicted all the way. The Met Officer advised flying up via the West Coast which had a reasonable cloud base, rather than the East Coast where 'all hell was let loose on the lee side of the Pennines'.

By 12.30 I was airborne in L 2201 with Wren Palmer and Warrant Officer Jock Bryce as Navigator. Jock Bryce had been with us some time and had proved himself a 'jack of all trades' and master of them all. On this day he was to assume an unexpected nautical role.

My forecast that this was going to be an unpleasant trip was confirmed as we wallowed past the clocktower on the Abberley Hills north of Malvern and Jock announced that we were only making 50 knots over the ground.

Although Wren Palmer was good on her comparatively untested radar, we had no conventional navigational aids. All we could do was to look over the side to see where we were, so we had to remain within sight of the ground as we crept northwards. This suited us as the nearer the ground we flew the less would be the windspeed. It seemed hours later that we crept past Runcorn and then out over the sea with Blackpool Tower to starboard.

I had originally envisaged flying over the Galloway Hills to Prestwick, then on through the valley of the Clyde to the Forth and so to Arbroath, but as we were passing Walney Island Jock said, 'we'll not be getting to Arbroath today if this wind keeps up. I reckon we'll be pushed to get to Prestwick by dark if our groundspeed remains the same. There'll be very little daylight after four o'clock in these high latitudes.'

It soon became obvious that it was going to be a coastal trip all the way to Prestwick, for the clouds were well down at St Bees Head and there was no question of taking a short cut over the Galloway Hills. They were already cloud covered, with clouds 'full of mountain'. So we altered course to fly up Wigtown Bay and on we droned towards Prestwick.

We were flying up the East side of Loch Ryan when we flew through a particularly vicious patch of turbulence, darkness was descending fast, the ground speed seemed infinitesimal and morale was at a low ebb. Down on my port side I could see Sunderland flying boats straining at their moorings in Wig Bay. We were in an amphibian. Why should we fly any further?

I tried to call Wig Bay on the frequencies which I carried but I obtained no reply. Not to worry, with the war-time requirement for constantly changing call signs and frequencies there was nothing unusual about not being able to make contact.

I decided to land while we still had some daylight and my decision seemed to be confirmed as the right one when on turning downwind on the front of a squall I found myself a mile to leeward of Wig Bay before I had completed my turn for an approach and landing into wind.

Jock Bryce hadn't flown in a Walrus before operating on water, but there is a first time for everything, so I explained to him that after we had landed I would put the wheels down to give us drag and reduce our taxiing speed, whereupon he was to go up forward into the forehatch and stand by with the painter to slip it through any part of the mooring buoy which I would approach as slowly as possible. He was then to bring the painter back aboard and make it fast. I would shut down the engine when he held his hand up to indicate that we were made fast. I would then moor up properly myself later on. That was what we intended.

Although the wind was screaming down the loch Wig Bay did enjoy a little shelter from a protruding headland and such was the speed of the wind that we settled on the water with negligible forward speed.

The only spare mooring, however, was up to windward. It would do, but in a single engined flying boat it is always preferable to choose a leeward mooring so that if things go wrong you don't drift back into other expensive moored aircraft.

Morale was high at this point. I had made the right decision. We were down after three hours in very rough air and the shades of night were falling fast, but there seemed to be a lack of marine craft around. We would have need of a tender, not only to take us ashore but in case we needed a tow. I also suddenly realised, but kept it to myself, that although we had the anchor cable on the drum we had no anchor. For our daily local flying at Defford ancillary equipment such as anchors and guns were not needed and had been placed in store. They were still there – in the store!

Still, why should we need an anchor? I had never known anyone use an anchor in an aircraft at a flying boat base. There were always marine craft around to give a tow in case of emergency.

With wheels down I crept up to the buoy 'blipping' the engine on the magneto switches to reduce taxiing speed to the minimum. With Jock Bryce mooring up for the first time in his life I didn't want to ram the buoy with too much speed on. Then I boobed. We were only ten feet from the buoy and I kept the switches off too long. The engine was still rotating but on switching on for the last 'blip' there was a ghastly silence. The engine died completely.

Still no marine craft appeared, and as I subsequently discovered this was not surprising as the duty crew were at tea prior to carrying out their last check on moored craft.

Meanwhile we were off downwind tail first at about four knots. The wheels were still down, which helped to reduce our speed of drift in the strong wind, but it was merely a matter of seconds before we should crash into the first Sunderland on the trot.

I could already visualise the questions at the coming Court of Enquiry. Why hadn't I flown to West Freugh south of Stranraer and landed on the airfield there? Why hadn't I checked on the frequencies and call signs of stations from which I might need help on the way? The most embarrassing question of all - why hadn't I checked that the anchor was aboard before departure? etc. etc.

Had the Walrus been a modern aircraft (it was of pre-war vintage) equipped with an electric starter I would merely have had to press a button to re-start the engine. There would have been no crisis. The Pegasus engine, however, was started by means of an incredible piece of Victoriana known as an inertia starter, best explained as being akin to an agricultural cream separator. With the best will in the world at least 25 to 30 seconds were required to activate this starter. This was done by leaping out of the cockpit with the starting handle and clambering up on to the starboard lower mainplane where there was solid decking to stand on, on the starboard side of the engine. The handle was then inserted into the inertia starter and you started winding; very slowly at first, for the gearing between the handle and the flywheel of the inertia starter was such that one revolution of the handle equalled several hundred revolutions of the flywheel. Normally two people were able to turn the handle for a 'quick' start, but in our predicament only Wren Palmer was available. Luckily she was used to starting the Walrus and also used to flying with me - she was out of the cockpit without a word of command and had clambered up onto the decking and slowly building up revolutions in the inertia starter in a matter of seconds.

She was facing aft and no doubt the sight of the fast

80

approaching Sunderland and the trot behind us lent strength to her efforts.

I stood up in my cockpit, transfixed, awaiting the oncoming crash. I reckoned we were going to drive backwards into the Sunderland somewhere between the engines on the starboard wing. We were a small aircraft but our high biplane profile would never go under the Sunderland wing. Considerable destruction was inevitable, and yet such is human nature that in this crucial moment of impending doom and tension I was distracted by . . . woman.

Wren Palmer was a well built beautifully proportioned girl and it was a delightful spectacle to see her magnificent figure displayed in the ballet of the inertia starter. I forgot the impending crash into the Sunderland and merely wondered whether the weft and warp of her trouser seat would stand the pressures of the arabesque conché she performed on each downstroke of the massive starting handle.

Three seconds to go and ten feet from disaster she stopped turning, shouted contact and pulled the toggle which engaged the inertia starter with the main engine so that all the energy she had built up could be transferred.

As I turned round and dropped down into my seat the Pegasus engine fired and, joy of joys, at full throttle I taxied away from what would undoubtedly have been a courtmartial.

The screaming wind, the gathering dark and the lack of marine craft decided me to have no more truck with trying to moor up. Not all that far away was the slip used normally for bringing the Sunderlands out of the water on their cradles. We were an amphibian. Why not drive her out of the water and up the slip on her wheels?

It meant taxiing cross wind – a difficult thing to do in a Walrus in a strong wind, for like all flying boats the Walrus had an inbuilt desire to weathercock.

We built up plenty of speed and rushed at the slip. We needed the speed not only to counter the cross wind, but to get up to the top of the slip. As we approached, an airman, the first we had seen, rushed down with his arms above his head giving the signal to stop. I wasn't stopping. Subsequently I discovered that he meant well. He didn't know that we were an amphibian with our wheels down below the surface of the water, and he thought we ought to wait for a cradle to bring us out!

We rushed the slip in fine style keeping the power on to make sure we reached the top, only to discover that the main Stranraer to Kirkcolm road ran across the top of the slip and that we were about to dispute the right of way on the main road with a civilian lorry hurrying to Kirkcolm. But yet another collision was avoided. We crossed the road and found enough space to park the Walrus amongst some oil drums. We lashed her wings down to concrete blocks, chocked her wheels and left her snug for the coming winter's night.

Wren Palmer was accommodated in a remote nissen hut with the WAAFs. They told us she was lucky not to have slept in their accommodation a week earlier, when the WAAFs had awakened in the half light of dawn to find two three-week old calves in their sleeping accommodation! Two members of the marine craft unit passing the WAAF hut in the pre-dawn light had come across the two calves loose in the lane. Being possessed of a sense of humour they cajoled the calves into the WAAF sleeping accommodation then retired behind a bank on the roadside to await developments. They weren't disappointed. Soon some of the occupants were baling out into the Scottish dawn in their Wincyette service issue pyjamas, while two girls with an agricultural background solved the problem!

As usually happens after a gale the next day dawned with blue skies and an inviting and scintillating Loch Ryan.

We refuelled the Walrus ashore, started up and waddled down the slip into the loch. After taxiing around to warm up and testing magnetos on full power it was wheels up and take off on a two hour enjoyable flight to Arbroath.

I flew many other flights in Walrus aircraft but never another without an anchor.

The 15th January 1943 was cold, bitterly cold. An Arctic airstream blew down the British isles from the North West. A Walrus amphibian, L 2201, powered by its single pusher Pegasus engine, slowly wallowed her way against the turbulent headwind bound for RAF Ballykelly in Northern Ireland from RAF Defford in the heart of Worcestershire.

Unknown to the military members of her crew her mission was to have a profound effect on the Battle of the Atlantic.

Only TRE could have despatched such a disparate crew in a Royal Naval Aircraft to the Land of Saints and Martyrs.

Although an RAF officer I was the pilot of this Naval aircraft and I was accompanied by a woman radar operator, Wren Knight, an RAF Signaller, Flight Sergeant Nutt, a civilian photographer, Douglas Fisher, and, in overall charge of our party, Doctor A M Uttley, a Senior Scientific Officer of TRE.

Our mission was occasioned by the disappointing results being achieved by Coastal Command in their war against the 'U' boats. Aircraft were sighting 'U' boats on the surface but by the time they reached them the 'U' boats had disappeared leaving merely a slick to show where they had been. Attacking aircrews had only the haziest idea of where and when to drop their depthcharges once the 'U' boat had disappeared.

Air Chief Marshal Sir Philip Joubert, Commander in Chief, Coastal Command approached TRE at Malvern to help solve the problem. He asked the establishment if it could devise something which would enable bombaimers to be more accurate. Dr Uttley, who specialised in Optics, was asked to find a solution. All he could be given to go on was that a submarine submerging would continue on its approximate course in the same direction for 40 seconds but at a greatly reduced speed.

In due course he thought up an idea for a ground trainer in which aircrew sat on chairs with a bomb release button in their hands. Simulated attacks on submarines, submerging ahead of them, were made by means of a colour film projected onto a screen. When the aircrew pressed their button simulating the dropping of a depth charge a recording was made from which it was possible to estimate their undershoot or overshoot. It was a simple matter to calculate their errors and this training system enabled them to attain considerably better bombing results . . . until the 'U' boats decided to fight it out on the surface!

To make the film of the various types of attack to be projected in the trainer an 'H' class submarine, H 33, at Londonderry was placed at the Doctor's disposal and the Walrus was required to fly up to Ballykelly to carry out the photographic work. The photographer was Douglas Fisher, a TRE civilian. He was a dedicated photographer who flew several hundreds of hours with the Flying Unit and he was regarded as 'unofficial aircrew' for his interests were not solely confined to photography. Such was his enthusiam for aviation that he could navigate, work a radar set, act as Flight Engineer, fly the aircraft and land many of the unit's various types of aircraft under dual control. He obtained amazing photographic results often standing in open hatches exposed to the airstream and, like many TRE staff, was quite impervious to cold, discomfort and danger once he was concentrating on the task in hand. Fisher was perhaps hardier than most for he was on occasions airsick but it made no difference to his determination to attain good results. On the coming flights he would have to kneel in the bow position of the Walrus with his whole body from the waist upwards exposed to the wintry Atlantic weather.

While the aircraft carried out dizzy climbs and lightning swoops on the 'swirl' left by the dived submarine he would have to photograph each run up to the 'target' using a hand held 16 mm cine camera. All that would keep him from going

The outstanding success of British radar research could only have been achieved with quite remarkable leadership, for men of genius do not easily into a team nor are naturally amenable to discipline. This leadership was provided by Dr AP Rowe, Superintendent of TRE, here seen in his office, the headmaster's study at Malvern College. *Photo: Douglas Fisher*

Participators in a Sunday Soviet at the Telecommunications Research Establishment, Malvern, charged with the developing of radar as a weapon of war

Standing: AVM OGWG Lywood, A/Cdr GP Chamberlain, G/Cpt J Shepherd-Smith, G/Cpt GN Hancock, G/Cpt CA Bell, Prof DM Robinson, Mr CJ Carter, S/Ldr WH Thompson, G/Cpt CC Morton, Mr JC Duckworth, Mr EH Cook-Yarborough, Dr RA Smith, Mr AB Jones, Mr J Stewart, Dr AT Starr, Dr TC Keeley, Dr AH Cooke, G/Cpt JA Macdonald, Mr RJ Dippy, Dr DA Jackson

Sitting: A/Cdr WC Cooper, A/Cdr CS Cadell, A/Cdr WPG Pretty, Sir Robert Renwick, Lord Cherwell, AVM Sir Victor Tait, Mr AP Rowe, Mr DW Fry, A/Cdr CP Brown, AVM WE Theak, G/Cpt EC Passmore, Dr FC Williams, Mr C Holt Smith, A/Cdr MK Porter, Dr WB Lewis

At first sight not a particularly interesting picture but as the names reveal these were politicians, senior scientists and humble aircrew gathered together for one of Dr AP Rowe's informal chats on a Sunday morning throughout the war. In the old headmaster's study at Malvern College are the men who made the policy, the men who made the tools, the scientists, and the aircrew who used the tools. At these 'soviets' problems were thrashed out informally

5 May 1941. The Bucker aircraft stolen from the Germans by two young Frenchmen, Boudard and Hebert and flown to Christchurch in Hampshire

Douglas Fisher in the bow of the Walrus ready to take cine film of diving submarine. *Photo: AE Uttley*

Off Moville, Eire. Wren Knight throws heaving line to 'H' class submarine from Walrus. *Photo: Douglas Fisher*

over the side was a 'monkey chain' attached to the floor and clipped on to his parachute harness. This was just as well or we might have lost one of our major post war contributors to natural history films for television.

Three hours and thirty minutes after taking off from RAF Defford almost overcome by hypothermia, we landed at RAF Ballykelly.

With our circulation recovered, on the following day we visited the submarine base at Londonderry to discuss our requirements with the submarine commander Lieutenant M H Jupp DSC and his officers. The boat H 33 had only just come in from sea and to a stranger from another service a submarine just in from sea is militarily rather unusual. It is difficult to tell who is who because of the crew's bizarre clothing. Wearing their 'pirate dress' ranks are difficult to define. The crew know the ranks of course because they all know each other, but it is very hard to tell who is an officer and who is not and who is senior to whom. Furthermore everybody smells and the crew don't seem to notice the smell among themselves.

Amongst these milling pirates I felt a bit of a fool as I had put on my best uniform for this visit to the senior service.

It was a successful meeting and even the smell disappeared after a few pre-luncheon pink gins.

We arranged for H 33 to go out to sea each day; far enough out so that we would have no land in the background of our film. We required the submarine to execute dives, while Dr Uttley directed our attacks from various angles and distances and Fisher took his cine shots on each attack.

Due to the possible presence of 'U' boats neither the Walrus nor H 33 was to use radio at sea, so all signalling was to be done by lamp.

As it would be necessary to confer each morning about the day's programme before putting to sea, Jupp suggested that while he headed down Lough Foyle we should fly over to Moville on the West side of the lough and land on the water to await his arrival. There were moorings in the bay, he said, which we could pick up and there should be someone around who would ferry us over to H 33 in a dinghy to confer when he arrived off Moville.

The only snag about this proposal was that Moville was in a neutral country, Eire. Would we be running into trouble for violating Eire's territorial waters? If we applied to higher authority for permission there would be a considerable delay, after which the answer would certainly be 'No'. I saw how rugged and operational Jupp looked and felt we must show him that the Air Force was flexible. We arranged to meet at Moville the next morning at 0900 hours without embarrassing anybody by asking for permission.

During the ensuing pre-luncheon conversation First Lieutenant Wood said that he hoped we wouldn't be too long on our filming on the morrow as he was due for leave after duty and hoped to catch the night boat to Liverpool from Belfast the following evening.

In a fit of gin-induced euphoria and bonhomie I said, 'Not to worry; if the landing works at Moville in the morning and we are not arrested we'll land at Moville again in the afternoon and pick you up off H 33. It will save an hour's steaming up the lough and I may be able to fix you up an RAF flight to Prestwick.'

It was one of those 'gin promises' that seem all right at the time and which you regret afterwards.

Next day at 8.30 found the Walrus circling off Moville harbour. I was very careful not to infringe blatantly Irish neutrality by flying over the land. Then I alighted on the water and pumped down the landing wheels to reduce taxiing speed and we kept our eyes fixed on the shore to see if there was any reaction. An old man was loading a donkey cart with stones on the beach. He looked up once and then went on loading stones. There was no other reaction – no signalling, no flak, no shots across the bow. We took up a mooring on one of the outer buoys, cut the engine and waited for the sub.

We raised the wheels in case we had to taxi away quickly out of Eire's territorial water.

Presently a boat put out from the shore. Should we stay, risking arrest – the Curragh – internment for the duration – loss of an important scientist? – or make an undignified retreat? It was not a very smart looking boat and there was only one man in it. He was wearing a uniform cap – probably the Harbour Master. I decided to risk staying but sent Nutt and Wren Knight up onto the wing with the starting handle, just in case. You needed two people on the inertia starting handle for a quick start.

The man in the boat rested on his oars, just ahead of us and stayed there. Obviously he was crafty. He knew that I could only go forward if I wanted to get away and avoid arrest and it would mean ramming him. Then he leant forward and spoke. 'Would you be wanting any eggs?' he asked.

I invited him aboard. He was a lovely character with the typical Irish sense of humour and a great disrespect for all higher authority. I explained why we were there. The 'Harbour Master' made no pronouncement about the Walrus being in Irish territorial waters and he agreed to ferry Fisher, Dr Uttley and me over to the submarine, which was then steaming down the lough.

When the conference with the submarine commander was over we had time to spare. The Walrus hadn't to rendezvous at sea for another two hours. Meanwhile the 'Harbour Master' rowed ashore and returned with a case of 36 dozen eggs. Rationing in Ulster was not as strict as in England, but strict enough to render 432 eggs in one lump something of a portent. They were gratefully received by the messes at Ballykelly and at RAF Limavady.

The first day's filming went well and we flew back to Ballykelly leaving H 33 to carry out further training with a destroyer. In view of our successful landing at Moville in the morning we confirmed with H 33 that we would pick up Lt Wood at Moville in the afternoon at about 1630 hours.

Lieutenant G J Gellie, RANVR, would take over as 1st Lieutenant.

Although gin promises are sometimes unreliable, as luck would have it this one ticked and worked better than any sophisticated and powerful planning staff could have devised.

We confirmed that a Liberator (4 engined American-built bomber) would be leaving for Prestwick that evening from Ballykelly. There would be room for one Naval Officer aboard.

At 1600 hours we took off for the three minute flight to Moville.

In the morning we had mentioned to the 'Harbour Master' that we might land again in the late afternoon and sure enough as we taxied up to the mooring his boat could be seen rowing from the shore.

He arrived with *another* box of 36 dozen eggs in the bilges! We were in the egg business in a big way!

We transhipped the eggs placing them on the centre of gravity in the companionway alongside the signaller's compartment.

The 'Harbour Master' said he was happy to await H 33 and tranship our passenger from the sub to our Walrus. And wait we did. In those latitudes there is not a lot of daylight on the 25th January.

Nautical twilight came - still no submarine and only 15 minutes to take off for the Liberator. It was getting dark and it dawned on me that I had never flown a Walrus in the dark before, let alone taken off in the dark off water. Then the submarine appeared coming up the lough against the ebb with a bone in her teeth. She lost way and soon, in the gathering gloom, we could see the Harbour Master rowing at 40 strokes to the minute coming over to us. In the stern-sheets sat Lt Wood, DSC RNVR, wearing his peaked dress cap and best uniform. His hands were clasped ecclesiastically over his stick, held vertically between his knees. I had never seen him other than in a dirty white polo necked sweater and beret. It suddenly dawned on me that this was a formal occasion. I was receiving the First Lieutenant of one of her Majesty's warships on my craft! I pulled off my helmet and dived forward to the bow position with my peaked cap. The 'Harbour Master' backed in to the port side of the cockpit hatch. Fisher took Lt Wood's bag, Flight Sergeant Nutt stood stiffly to attention on the wing ready to start the engine, and as Wood stood on our 'deck' prior to descending into the cockpit we formally exchanged salutes, Wood solemnly holding his walking stick now in his left hand. The trickiest operation of a difficult day had been achieved with dignity and success.

It is an axiom that while rivalry may exist between the services the desire to try and be efficient and helpful when dealing with each other is natural to each service. I like to think that the Air Force possesses this attribute in possibly greater measure because it is the junior service.

This was now borne out. As Nutt wound the inertia starter I called Air Traffic Control and asked them if they would hold the Liberator. They said they would try to. Taxiing out into the mainstream I ran through take-off checks and glanced back. Lieutenant Wood was sitting on the box of 36 dozen eggs with his hands still clasped over his stick. He could not strap in as there wasn't a seat for him, but it was a smooth trip. Two and a half minutes later we were on the now dark runway at Ballykelly landing short just past the nose of the Liberator waiting to taxi on to the runway. A quick 180° turn and we unloaded Wood, who was unceremoniously hustled behind the whirring propellers and up into the bomb-bay entrance of the Liberator. Whoever was escorting him had the sense to grab the hat off his head before he lost it in the slipstream. As Wood disappeared into the maw of the Liberator he was still grasping his stick. I've often wondered why an officer should need a stick on a submarine. Some ancient naval tradition perhaps?

The drama was not yet finished. The Liberator pilot called Prestwick as soon as he was airborne and said he had a passenger for London. Prestwick offered to hold a Dakota for him which was then loading on the tarmac. Lieutenant T D Wood, DSC RNVR, landed at Hendon three and a half hours after leaving H 33's conning tower at Moville!

The meetings at Moville and the purchase of eggs became a daily routine. One day when the 'Harbour Master' didn't appear in time to do the ferrying I started up the engine and taxied over to the submarine. It was then that we found that the high, vertical sided bow of H 33 made an excellent place for the Walrus to push its nose into. As this procedure was repeated on later days the submarine crew became adept at receiving the flying boat and holding off the fragile wings with broom heads wrapped around with 'rags-cleaning'. After disembarking the Walrus would lay off 'windrode' at the end of a line. There was no chance of any damage. We also instilled in the matelots one of the golden rules of aviation – never throw a line from a ship to a flying boat. It should be the other way round because a very embarrassing situation can arise if a line is thrown into a flying boat's propeller. The pilot has to keep his engine or engines going by blipping the magneto switches to obtain low revolutions until he is made fast. The experience they gained was to prove of value later.

On the last day of the trials with only Douglas Fisher and Flight Sergeant Nutt as signaller, I joined the submarine as usual somewhere out in the Atlantic where she was to go through the manoeuvres which had been arranged. After diving and surfacing several times in an orthodox manner while we cruised overhead, H 33 to our amazement, suddenly broke surface in what could only be described as a climbing turn to port. She shot out of the sea at an angle of 45°, flopped back on the water and then started a wild left-handed circling. As she lost way sailors poured out of the hatch and ran aft along the hull, finally peering into the sea over the port quarter.

This was a most unorthodox performance, not called for in our script. Having seen H 33 break surface many times in recent days we realised that something must be drastically wrong. I continued cruising round, wondering what happened next. The Atlantic was unnaturally calm for midwinter, and perhaps slightly sinister. From our height of about 500 feet we could just see the misty outline of the Donegal mountains away to the south-east.

Soon she called up on the lamp: AAA AM DAMAGED CANNOT PROCEED SUGGEST YOU RETURN TO BASE A R. We acknowledged and then swooped low to have a closer look. Something seemed to be stuck under the port quarter, and a seaman was jumping up and down on it up to his waist in the icy waters of the Atlantic.

I climbed again to 500 feet and flew in a wide circle, thinking. Was this an emergency to justify breaking radio silence? I could call up Ballykelly; or I might fly back and report, rather inadequately, what had happened. On the other hand here was a golden opportunity to land on the sea and find out exactly what the trouble was. Everything seemed propitious for that ultimate desire of all flying boat captains, an open sea landing – successful if possible. Certainly the winter Atlantic would never be in a better mood.

My passion for the sea and ships was too much for me and I fell for it. I made a good landing, the swells, although lumpy, being too far apart to have much effect on the Walrus. I had no qualms about going alongside because the submarine's crew were now well experienced in handling the Walrus in the more sheltered waves of Lough Foyle. With wheels down for drag I blipped the motor and pushed our bow against his port-side forward of the conning tower. Douglas Fisher threw the painter and two seamen held off the wings with brooms. Then I cut the engine. Flight Sergeant Nutt opened the hatch and we scrambled out onto the hull of the submarine to confer.

H 33 was now twenty five years old, having been built in 1918. It appeared that the deck plating which housed the mooring ropes and provided a level walkway had deteriorated with the years. During the last dive at full speed this deck casing had torn off on the port-side and, acting as an elevator-cum-rudder, had played havoc with the controls. As she was diving at full speed, the effect had been as violent for the crew as it was spectacular for the Walrus, and we found we were talking to a somewhat shaken submarine Captain.

The Chief Engine Room Artificer reckoned that it would take about an hour to cut away the damaged plating, after which they might be able to proceed, but on the surface only. (The Royal Navy, though they can sail, steam or make way, prefer to 'proceed'; it is a more formal kind of motion appropriate to the Senior Service). There would certainly be no more demonstration dives for a while, but luckily we had just about completed our programme.

We were invited to lunch, and as we were not due back at Ballykelly for at least two and a half hours, I accepted gladly. By delaying our departure we would be better able to report at base if the repairs weren't completed when we had to leave.

The matelots laid the Walrus off on a 30 fathom line with a watch on deck to see that she came to no harm. The submarine lay in its own little world on the long oily swell; no land was in sight at that level and the sun could just be seen through high overcast. The loneliness and utter stillness seemed somewhat ominous, and the thought crossed my mind that we were a sitting duck for any 'U' boat prowling around. A working party was starting with sledgehammers, chisels and giant wire-cutters as we went down to the hatch for lunch.

We enjoyed a convivial meal, with bangs and thumps reverberating through the hull. The food, as always on operational craft, was much better than was provided by shore messes. We had reached the coffee stage when the Chief ERA reported that H 33 was ready to proceed.

When I climbed the conning tower to the bridge I was horrified to find the wind blowing at about force 3 to 4, and the waves beginning to break. It is always difficult to judge weather conditions inside a submarine, the large amount of hull submerged making it less susceptible to surface waves. The conditions I found would have been a mere nothing to seamen or yachtsmen; but for an aviator wishing to get a flying boat airborne they were approaching the impossible. The submarine was making a fine breakwater for the Walrus, which lay comfortably in her lee. Weathercocked, she looked perfectly happy sitting there. But I knew that my love of 'messing about in boats' had, not for the first time, landed me in a spot.

With the wind freshening all the time I explained my problem to Jupp and Gellie as we stood in the lee of the conning tower. If the Walrus hit a breaking wave before I had proper flying control she would be thrown in the air, then stall and fall back into the sea and probably wreck herself; or she might start porpoising – though that could be cured and a fresh start made.

Jupp offered to tow us back to Lough Foyle, but I quailed at the mere thought; a tow from the Navy in my experience, be it in yacht or flying boat, always ended in disaster. The trouble is that the Navy are not conscious of their power; to them 'taking it slowly' means about 15 knots, so that you are banged about on the surface like a mackerel on a line; or alternatively they let in the clutch (or whatever makes a ship move) with such abandon that they tow your bitts off the foredeck, leaving you wallowing forlornly and trying to keep the sea from rushing into your broken bows.

It was well worth having a shot at a take-off first.

A more hopeful course was that H 33 should make a 'slick' for us which she could do by steaming off up wind at full speed and bashing the seas flat while I waited astern of her; then when she had got far enough ahead I would chase after her in the smooth water of the slick and try to get airborne without hitting her. The principle of making a slick had been used for years by big ships, but probably never before by a submarine; and there was a nagging doubt whether a submarine could make one wide enough for the Walrus.

I was unhappily aware that this was one of those cases where if things went wrong it would mean a court martial. Their Lordships (the Admiralty) and Their Airships (the Air Council) took the poorest possible view of those who broke aeroplanes in this kind of lark. On the other hand a successful take-off would be regarded as a good show. This was one of the hazards of military life which must be accepted. No wonder Napoleon, or was it Lincoln, in considering the promotion of an officer, would ask, 'Is he lucky?'

Jupp agreed to have a go. Remembering my first open sea take-off in a Walrus with Stanley Adams I explained that I was interested in rescue operations if things went wrong. The Walrus was to take position 100 yards down wind of H 33, and when I signalled with the Aldis lamp, the sub would dash off up wind at full speed to cut the slick. I would have to judge how much start to give her; if I gave too much the slick would be nullified and I would be starting in rough water; if I gave too little I would probably hit the submarine before I was airborne.

The sailors hauled in the Walrus and we all emplaned. I taxied a couple of hundred yards downwind in the rough water and then let her weathercock into the wind. H 33 had vanished!

When the next swell lifted us I saw her again. I tried a fast taxi towards her and everything was blotted out with the water pouring over windscreen and hatch. It was some consolation to think that the Walrus was the best flying boat ever made for taking off in a rough sea – a Sunderland would never have had a hope in those conditions.

When we were 100 yards behind H 33 we gave the signal for him to 'proceed'. Now was the moment! I was thankful that on this our last filming Wren Knight and Doc Uttley weren't aboard; we were that much lighter, and if things went badly the fuss wouldn't be so great if a woman and a top scientist weren't involved.

100 yards, 200, 300 and then the submarine vanished in the long Atlantic swell. I knew that as soon as I opened the throttle I would see nothing but water cascading over the top of the fuselage and hissing through all the slits and cracks of the cockpit hatch. Fortunately the sun was visible to starboard and helped me to keep direction. I pulled the throttle override 'cheese-cutter', opened up and we roared over the crest of the first swell and I could see the submarine going up the slope of the next one ahead – unpleasantly close. We went down the swell, and the flying controls began to come alive. Things weren't going too badly. As soon as we were at the bottom of the swell the sub had vanished again. We got to the top of the next one . . . and we were airborne. As the cascading water finally cleared from the windscreen I could see H 33 just going under the starboard wing, while Jupp, Gellie and a signaller in the conning tower waved in a happy, relaxed, confident manner. Had they but known!

Oh the joy of rocketing into the friendly air after wrenching yourself, against the odds, from the powerful hold of Gravity! We thundered round H 33 at nought feet, did a tight turn round the conning tower in sheer bravado, and set course for Moville.

This was to be our last landing at Moville for our task was done and on the next day we were to return to more mundane work at RAF Defford.

So at Moville we loaded up with our last box of eggs and a dozen pairs of silk stockings, said goodbye to our friendly 'Harbour Master' and made our last water take-off.

On the following day, the last in January, 1943, we loaded up ourselves, our baggage, our eggs, our stockings and many loaves of soda bread and flew back to Defford.

It had been an interesting and unusual detachment and

happily it achieved the results for which Coastal Command craved.

Poor Jupp. He didn't survive the war. When in command of the submarine *Syrtis* his boat is presumed to have hit a mine off Bodo, Norway, at the end of March, 1944.

In mid-April 1943 came more waterwork with the Walrus. This time in the Menai Straits, North Wales. Two other pilots were to be trained for flying the Walrus off water. Lieutenant Commander A E Milward who now joined the unit to command the Naval Section and Flight Lieutenant Jimmy Proctor, a very colourful individual who was usually accompanied in flight by his Spaniel dog 'Pimple'. Pimple came with us for this training.

In glorious spring weather, which lasted for several days, we flew over to the Straits from Defford each morning. While there was no RAF station at Menai, flying boat moorings were laid in the Straits opposite Cadnant Creek for the use of boats flown in to Saunders Roe who had a factory about a mile and a half from the moorings at Beaumaris. It was an ideal area for our purpose. No other aircraft flying, little water traffic and only one Sunderland moored on the end mooring of a trot of six so we were able to practise picking up moorings with the minimum risk of collision. Even more so than land based aircraft flying boats are very attracted to each other and will snuggle up to each other when the opportunity offers.

On the first day, when it came to lunchtime, we landed, picked up a mooring and switched off. The verdant beauty of the Straits, the silence, the sun, scenery, scintillating wavelets and utter peace after enduring the noise of the Pegasus engine held us enthralled.

We were about to tuck into the unexpired portion of the day's rations perched on the hull and lower mainplanes enjoying the sun when a man rowed over to us from a yacht nearby called *Perula*. *Perula* was owned by a Mr & Mrs

Adams who had sailed to Spitzbergen in her before the war. Mr Adams asked us over to have drinks and soup on *Perula* and eat our lunch aboard. It turned out that Mrs Adams was formerly Miss Winifred Brown who had won the Kings Cup Air Race before the war, hence her compassion for us fellow aviators.

It was a most convivial occasion and it was some time before we could tear ourselves away to start the afternoon's training.

Not only did the challenge and thrill of flying boat handling impress Milward and Procter but the beauties of the Straits and the hospitality of the Adams, repeated on subsequent days, made the conversion course a very pleasant wartime interlude.

I had no objection to enjoying the smooth when it was offered. I didn't believe in creating the rigours of war; they were only too ready to create themselves and the time was now due for I was to leave TFU and join a very odd outfit indeed, No 138 Special Duty Squadron at RAF Tempsford.

CHAPTER 7

Landings

And so in April 1943 I went to war with 138 Squadron flying Halifax aircraft from RAF Tempsford in Bedfordshire.

This was one of the two squadrons which, during moon periods, flew exclusively for SOE (Special Operations Executive) taking men and supplies to the Resistance units in Norway, Poland, Belgium, Holland, France and occasionally, even agents to Germany and Austria.

My career with 138 Squadron was cut short on the night of 14/15th August 1943 when I was shot down flying low over Annecy in Haute Savoie, France. I was lucky for I was the sole survivor of my crew, saved by being propelled through the windscreen into telephone wires.

I spent more hours walking than flying with this squadron and it was Christmas 1943 before I got back to England via the Pyrenees and Gibraltar.*

What made this incident so embarrassing is that after the war, when visiting Annecy, I was informed that I had been shot down by an Italian Alpini Corporal with a small Beretta machine pistol who was on guard duty at the entrance to Annecy Barracks. To add insult to injury I was told that before the war he had been a waiter at Sestriere! I didn't

------

* see 'Winged Hours' published by William Kimber 1981.

mind his being a waiter, an honourable and respected profession in Europe, but it was humiliating as an officer to be shot down by an NCO.

On return to England it was back to the boffins at the Telecommunications Flying Unit at RAF Defford, there to take part in one of the longed-for developments in aviation: the Automatic Landing of Aircraft.

To explain what this project involved it is necessary to go back a few years; or perhaps it would be better to glance back at pre-history, when the British climate became what it is today – one in which fog and low cloud prevail more than in any other European country, especially in winter.

During the early part of the war bombers caught out by bad weather after operations over Europe made use of various aids to landing, none of which were really satisfactory. One system, known as Lorenz Approach, was an aural method of detecting the line of approach to the runway through earphones; an experienced pilot with time on his hands to check his whereabouts in relation to the beam, and provided he wasn't too tired, could make a reasonable approach and land if visibility was reasonable. It could not handle more than one aircraft every five minutes. In war it was quite useless due to the large numbers involved.

Another system was to obtain frequent bearings from our vhf WAAF operators. Here the girls did a magnificent job but they really couldn't handle more than three aircraft at a time.

As the war developed navigators found that they could manage a reasonable approach to the runway in use by using their own 'Gee' navigational equipment. Again reasonable visibility, to make the actual landing, was required.

Towards the end of the war a system called Ground Controlled Approach, which had been developed in the United States, came into use. It was good. Any fool could use it if he could talk to the ground and could carry out the orders they gave him; but here again only a very few GCAs were available and they could not cope with large numbers of tired, recently-frightened pilots often in damaged aircraft and short of fuel all trying to get priority for a landing.

Such is human nature that a degree of one-upmanship developed to obtain priority for any form of assisted landing and that was to call up and give exaggerated details of the aircraft's condition. Arriving on three engines was insufficient disability for a priority landing but a call with the right intonation informing Control that you were on two engines would usually get priority treatment and an immediate landing. The story goes that at one airfield a pilot was almost lynched on the ground for, on hearing the home-coming bombers' woes over the radio, he said he was on one engine. This was true as he was flying a Hurricane which only had one engine anyway. He obtained priority over everyone else but this was considered in very bad taste.

No system provided all that was needed for 'blind' approaches, followed hopefully by a landing. Guidance about direction, distance to go and angle of glide were all required to take the aircraft safely on to the runway. They were not all available and owing to the inadequacy of the aids available the best that could be done for an aircraft wishing to land in bad visibility was to divert it to an aerodrome where the visibility was better. For this purpose three master airfields, called by the aircrew 'crashstrips' were made available on the East Coast. These were provided with enormously long and wide runways. Alongside these runways were trenches in which perforated pipes were sunk. In time of fog, vast quantities of a low grade fuel were pumped into these pipes, which was then set alight. This was the FIDO – the fog dispersal system — and it worked. Its glow could be seen on the final approach and such was the heat given off that the fog really did disperse.

Fido served its purpose at great cost for its fuel consumption was considerable. The disadvantage to a crew landing a damaged bomber with leaky fuel tanks, unknown damage to the undercarriage and maybe a hung up bomb was the fear that they might swing over the flames during their landing run. Landing in these conditions certainly kept the adrenalin flowing in the veins of the aircrew!

A fresh urgency was given to the blind landing problem when the American Airforce arrived. They thought that the English climate was atrocious and some thought it safer flying over Germany than trying to land at English airfields. They had little use for the blind landing aids so far invented.

Early in 1944 a team came from the United States to demonstrate a new system of assisted landing known then as Signals Corps System 51, subsequently abbreviated to ILS (Instrument Landing System).

This team was headed by a Lieutenant Colonel Francis L Moseley, formerly development engineer for the Sperry Company and largely responsible for ILS and his assistant Frank B Brady who had worked with Moseley for some time.

From these trials of ILS great things were to develop.

ILS was good and it did work, and it could handle aircraft far quicker than any previous system. It was fairly simple and easy to use from the pilot's point of view. Just two needles, one hanging vertically which told the pilot to turn left or right to line up with the runway and another normally horizontal which moved up and down and gave the pilot his angle of glide.

There is an ecclesiastical saying that a prophet is never honoured in his own country and so it was with Francis Moseley, for he had dreamed up an idea that was so obvious it is extraordinary that no one else had thought about it.

In the simplest terms, if by turning one knob on the autopilot you could make an aircraft go up and down, or by turning another knob make the aircraft turn left or right and if the ILS instrument on the instrument panel told the pilot to turn left or right or go up or down, why not join the autopilot to the instrument and let the autopilot do the work! It was as simple as that.

Moseley made up a coupling circuit on a breadboard* in the cellar of his house at Osborne, Ohio with just four wires hanging from it; two to the autopilot and two to the instrument but at his own base at Wright Field no one would let him try it out. He brought the basic bits to England from the States packed in his personal luggage. At RAF Defford he was most impressed at the happy go lucky carefree atmosphere and lack of rigid control. Just the soil in which new ideas could germinate.

After he'd been at Defford about a week demonstrating in our usual atrocious winter weather how the American ILS worked he asked if he could wire up his breadboard to the autopilot and ILS instrument in our Liberator (4 engined Bomber) to see whether the autopilot would bring the aircraft down the beam to the runway automatically.

I detailed Tom Stewart to take him up and after a quick lunch he was airborne. An hour later Tom Stewart came into the flight office, his helmet thrown back off his head, his parachute over his shoulder. He slumped into a chair. He looked as though he'd seen a ghost.

'What happened?' I asked. 'Did Moseley nearly kill you?'

'Good lord, no. The darn thing worked first time, and second and third! Moseley just sat beside me with the breadboard on his lap and an unlit cigar between his fingers. As we approached the centre line of the beam somewhere near Tewkesbury I put in the autopilot and we came slap down the beam on to the centre line of the runway. I could have let her go right on to the concrete had I wanted to. It's uncanny! It makes a better approach than I can do myself and what's more, we did it three times in all without any breakdowns or smell of burning.' (TRE pilots frequently experienced small electrical fires when trying out new equipment. The boffins never seemed to mind but, to the aircrew who were conscious

---

* A breadboard is the radio man's name for the piece of wood on which he mounts his basic equipment.

of the high octane fuel tanks surrounding them, a smell of burning could be embarrassing).

And so in February 1944 Automatic Landing of Aircraft as we know it today was born. Next day I tried it out myself. All that Tom Stewart said was true and then our station commander 'Old Mac' came into the picture.

Then aged 46 Group Captain J A McDonald, CBE, AFC, to give him his full title, was a Scot, a 1914/18 pilot who had specialised in radio. His accent was so strong it was difficult to understand him on the ground. In the air with 8000 horse power of engines roaring in your ears it was almost impossible. When I flew with him I usually arranged to detail a navigator called Jock Bryce, who was also a Scotsman, to come with us. I'd flown with Jock Bryce a lot and I could understand him on the intercom. Jock Bryce would listen to what Old Mac said and if I didn't get it first time he would repeat it. For some reason we were all slightly afraid of Old Mac. It was partly his size and appearance and partly that he spoke in a very loud voice, clipping the last syllable off his word-d-d-s-s-s. He was a good disciplinarian, and popular with the pilots, for he insisted on flying everything.

But he really hadn't the time to study fully the handling notes of the fifty various aircraft types which he flew. This gave me some concern, but on dual equipped aircraft it wasn't so bad. As I cowered in the right hand seat I could push or pull the odd lever he had forgotten, change the fuel tanks etc while Mac did the flying. He was only interested in the throttles, the flaps and the wheels! With single pilot aircraft it was somewhat riskier – for Mac.

One of the most difficult aircraft to fly on the station was one of our Naval Aircraft – an American Corsair. It was short and fat; had an engine so powerful that in effect the propeller wanted to stay stationary and turn the fuselage round instead. It was designed solely as an efficient naval aircraft to operate from an aircraft carrier. As soon as you opened the throttle it would dash off to starboard no matter how much rudder you put on, and on landing it would touch down and immediately shoot off to starboard again unless the tail wheel was locked centrally. On take off we used to keep the locked tail down as long as possible to help the steering and it was lethal to land with the tailwheel unlocked. On landing on an aircraft carrier it didn't matter because the arrester wire would keep the aircraft straight.

A chill struck my heart on the morning that Mac announced 'I'll fly the Corsair-r-r-r this afternoon. Have it ready at 2 o'clock and will you show me the taps before I go.'

I sent the Pilots Handling Notes to his office hoping that he would have time to study them before casting himself into the heavens.

At 1400 hours he appeared in his flying suit looking like a benign teddy bear, the handling notes sticking out of his knee pocket.

'I've read the notes. Where's the aeroplane?' he announced as though it should have been brought to his office.

After he had done up his straps I leant over him and gave him a rundown on the various controls and I emphasised how essential it was to ensure that the tailwheel was locked on takeoff and especially on landing. Mac roared off into the wide blue yonder.

We watched, not from the control tower, which was in a vulnerable position out on the airfield but from an underground air raid shelter at the side of the airfield.

His take off and landing were perfect!

When he came into the office to sign the Authorisation Book as having completed his detail he said 'Och, you young fellers don't know you're born-n-n. I'll admit she does swing a bit but in the early twenties I flew off aircraft carriers with no brakes and only a tailskid. I don't know what you're fussing about!'

But we loved Old Mac despite his bark and so did the airmen.

In the middle of the night he would appear in the

maintenance hangar when some panic work was going on. He would climb up on to a servicing platform where a fitter would be struggling against sleep and an inaccesible oil filter, and encourage him with some cogent Scottish expression ending with the word 'laddie'. The lower echelons of the other ranks were always addressed as 'laddie' when he was pleased.

And with Group Captain J A McDonald at Defford we had just the right man with the initiative, contacts, drive, political knowledge and native cunning; for cunning was needed, to sell 'Automatic Landings' to the powers that be.

And there was opposition. RAE Farnborough were jealous because we were achieving our automatic approaches with a continuous wave system and there was an unwritten understanding that TRE should only deal with pulse systems (radar) while RAE Farnborough should concentrate on continuous wave systems (radio). Furthermore though we were losing aircraft in great numbers because we couldn't get down in bad weather conditions, Farnborough had not produced any better system than the archaic German Lorenz beam with which the RAF bombers were already equipped. But even with a fresh pilot the Lorenz system could only handle a very few aircraft per hour and with over a thousand bombers returning from Germany on murky nights, Lorenz approaches were futile. Our bombers found they could do better trying to find the runway using their navigational aid 'Gee' or getting a 'ZZ' approach on vhf given by our WAAF wireless operators.

Indeed the British weather had so appalled the United States Air Force when they first came to Britain that a high level request had been made to the States for the production of a landing aid. This requirement was issued on a high priority. Moseley's visit with the ILS was the result.

Francis L Moseley not only had an agile brain but phenomenal powers of observation. These attributes were accompanied by a manner of speech that was succinct and convincing. His laconisms were not only astute and mirthmaking but instructive, never offensive and frequently opened my eyes to many of our inefficiencies as a nation brought about by our insularity, worship of tradition and our wealth.

We each enjoyed a single room in the same hut on No 7 dispersed site. Francis maintained that these huts were designed for maximum heat loss being of single brick construction with asbestos roofs. This was understandable. There was a war on and this was the cheapest and quickest building that could be provided. What irked Francis was the heating.

He could not understand why we, the British, who had invented the British Thermal Unit, had so few of them and why we seemed to design our heating systems to waste them.

He pointed out that in our present VIP accommodation each individual room was heated by a cast iron coal stove which was built to last a thousand years and was fitted internally with a firebrick lining to prevent any heat radiating from the stove into the room. To ensure the stove's further inefficiency the pipe from the back of the stove was taken straight through the wall and up the outside of the building. This ensured that the stove pipe gave off its heat to the Worcestershire countryside and not to the room it was meant to be heating! He was right of course and it is strange that our architects hadn't spotted this appalling inefficiency in the thousands of huts so constructed.

But while Francis never enjoyed the 70° Fahr he was used to in the USA he was luckier than many for I had by chance 'come by' an extra source of BTUs by courtesy of the Great Western Railway. This extra source of supply worried my conscience a little in that it smacked of the 'seemier side of private enterprise' and it could also perhaps be classified as 'conduct prejudicial to good Air Force Discipline'.

It happened in this way. A farmer, Hayden Jenkins, of

Pirton Court Farm which was not far from the airfield at Defford, not only invited officers and airmen alike from the station to partake of his patrimony in the form of gargantuan and beautifully cooked meals by his wife Gwen but on occasions we were invited to take part in some rough shooting. One day we were standing on the bank of the railway cutting which went through Pirton Combe Wood. We were each standing with a couple of shot rabbits in our free hand when a goods train chugging asthmatically uphill towards Worcester wheezed to a standstill beside us.

The driver shut off steam and called out in a strong Birmingham accent 'Oil swop yo sum cowl for a brace of them rabbits.'

Hayden agreed – handed up the rabbits and a shower of best anthracite was thrown off the tender on to the bank.

'Wear shururt of meat in Brum' said the driver. 'I come up this way Tuesdays. If ewe hang a couple of rabbits on that there tree when you've got any oil chuck ewe some cool.'

And from that day forth we were never short of best Welsh anthracite! There were plenty of rabbits about.

A salve to my conscience regarding this arrangement was the thought that some well deserving folk in Birmingham living on bare wartime rations were getting supplementary nourishment while American scientists, still rather shaken by having to share the hardships of the fifth winter of the war with the indigenous natives, were at least kept a little warmer.

Hayden Jenkins was a real son of the soil. He spoke with a delightful Worcestershire burr, was a first class farmer and a real countryman whose knowledge of the world was confined to the Vale of Evesham. Many years later I thought I would impress him by asking him over to RAF Abingdon to see the newly introduced Beverley Aircraft. The Beverley was big; at that time the largest in service in the RAF. It could carry a bus in its vast cargo hold with passengers on the upper deck.

I encouraged Hayden to mount the passenger steps with me, flung open the door to the vast cavern of the hold and said

'What do you think of that? Big isn't it?' I waited for his reply while he surveyed the vast interior and expected some appreciation with regard to the size of the freight compartment and the miracles of modern aviation.

All he said after a long pause was 'It would hold a hell of a lot of hay wouldn't it?'

It made me realise how one's outlook on life is so influenced and governed by one's profession! I felt rather humble.

Poor Hayden, he was to die in tragic circumstances shortly afterwards but through him we kept warm!

Francis L Moseley finally left to induct the American Forces in the United Kingdom in the use of ILS and surreptitiously to show how easy it was to make the system automatic.

Meanwhile old Mac set about trying to sell Automatic Approaches (and eventually Landings) to the Royal Air Force and Civil Aviation.

As a station communications aircraft we had an old 1931 twin engined Boeing 247, an ex United Airlines aircraft and the only one of its kind in Europe. This monoplane was beloved of pilots. It had a retractable undercarriage, a new feature in aircraft of its day. This was its only complexity. There were no flaps or other aerodynamic trimmings such as slots etc. It could be brought in 'over the hedge' at 55 knots with 2 pilots and ten passengers. It was certainly one of the safest aircraft ever produced and its performance, reliability and ease of handling is said to have been the reason for the rapid expansion of air travel in the early thirties in the United States.

We couldn't have had a better aircraft for the implementation of Mac's plan. He didn't want to write a paper on how Automatic Approaches and Landings could be achieved and then have it pigeon-holed, as so often happened. He wanted to give practical demonstrations and show that the system really worked before submitting a paper suggesting that research should be undertaken with the object of adopting the American Instrument Landing System, Moseley's 'black box' and electric autopilots, in the Royal Air Force and Civil Aviation. So invitations were sent out to all who should be indoctrinated to come to Defford and see a practical demonstration of Automatic Landing actually working. And they came and were impressed, not only by its performance when using the ILS but also by an automatic homing and orbitting device designed by a radar officer of unusual capability and potential. Flying Officer LC Barber was of course known as 'Figaro'. He was no ordinary radar officer. He had taken his degree at London University in Chemistry and I think research was in his blood for he soon devised his own black box for smoothing out radar signals and feeding them into the autopilot so we could demonstrate 'hands off' flying to the airfield, orbitting at any given mileage, finding the landing beam and then coming down the landing path in its own Boeing 247D stately manner. Because it was flapless and had to have a very low approach angle it could land without 'flare out'. I think it was the only aircraft which could do this in Europe at the time and this was a feature of the aircraft's design, not of its landing system. We were just lucky to have the placid Boeing.

Stewart and I had fitted her up with a blind flying hood for the first pilot and we became confident at bringing her in on automatics completely blind with whoever was safety pilot sitting in the co-pilots seat to check visually.

We would have liked to do a fog landing but of course the fog wouldn't oblige. So we hit on the idea of carrying out a completely automatic landing at night without lights. It was easy to arrange as the blackout restrictions were still enforced (January 1945).

This idea turned into a humiliating fiasco and really impressed me with the difficulty of overcoming man's natural instincts.

We clambered into the sky on that moonless January night fully confident of our ability to home automatically from a distance, orbit the airfield and come sedately down the approach beam in the normal Boeing fashion. A rumble of wheels on the runway would be the first we would know that we had arrived.

It was not to be. When the radio altimeter read 100 feet above the ground my nerves wouldn't stand the twitch any longer. I just had to switch on the wing landing light only to find that, as usual, we were exactly where we should be and the runway was straight ahead. It was obvious that either some ground reference was required such as the glow of Fido in fog or that the pilot, on selecting final approach, should be able to anaesthetise himself with a hypodermic needle! And so it was with all of us who flew the Boeing – we couldn't face landing in utter darkness.

It was an interesting experiment and possibly not relevant today with high intensity lighting offering some form of ground reference to remove the final approach 'twitch' element.

But before we were to win the political battle to get a development programme for Auto landings we almost lost Old Mac, and without Mac automatic landings might have been delayed a further ten or twenty years.

It seemed to be a normal morning until the station public address system announced 'Will Wing Commander Flying please contact Air Traffic Control immediately.' Whenever I heard this announcement the adrenalin would start coursing through my veins for it always heralded an aerial drama and all who heard also knew. Airmen would appear at hangar doors and administrators peer from their office windows.

I dashed into Air Traffic Control to be informed that RAF St Athan (west of Cardiff) had phoned to say that one of our Spitfires had twice tried to land there but had failed because it had no rudder! And the Spitfire was flown by our Station Commander Mac whose intended destination had been RAF

Brawdy (south west of Fishguard). It was an amazing piece of news because Station Commanders never lose their rudders.

For sheer speed of take off nothing exceeds a technical officer when an aerial drama takes place and so it was in this case. Breathlessly the Senior Technical Officer entered the control room grasping the Spitfire's Form 700 (the Form 700 contains every detail of every adjustment or replenishment of an aircraft from its birth to its death). It showed that the Spitfire had been fitted with a new rudder the previous day. Meanwhile Mac, having failed to land at St Athan, was heading back to us at Defford. Soon he came through on the R/T 'Is the Wing Commander Flying there?'

I answered and he told me that he just couldn't control the aircraft directionally at low approach speeds, that he had tried at RAF St Athan, that he was now at 9000 feet, having had a bad time climbing up through the clag.* Then came the 64 dollar question. 'What are the chances of landing this thing?'

I knew they were slight. The high landing speed and the impossibility of keeping directional control would undoubtedly lead to him hitting something. At Defford it might mean hitting experimental aircraft. Even if he could reach the crash strip on the East Coast at Woodbridge he would undoubtedly swing off and hit the trees; furthermore his fuel was already low. Aircraft were expendable (though dangerous when let loose over a populous island) but pilots, especially Group Captains, were not. With uneasy premonitions of the coming Court of Enquiry, which would probably, having plenty of time to spare, think up some obvious solution which hadn't occurred to me, I decided that I must advise Mac to bale out.

I knew he was fairly close to us by the strength of his transmissions and told him I thought his chances of landing successfully were nil and suggested that he should turn the

---

* Clag – RAF for 'cloud solid from top to bottom'

aircraft on to a course of 270° in the hope that it might land in the sparsely populated area of the Black Mountains.

There was a pause. I could imagine Old Mac weighing up the situation. He couldn't leap over the side of a £20,000 aircraft (1944 valuation) without a twinge of conscience any more easily than he could leap into it.

Presently he came through on the R/T, 'OK Griff' (the first time he had ever used my agnomen) 'I'm on 270°, height 9000 feet. What drill do you suggest?'

Here I was on firm ground having made such a hash of trying to bale out of my Hurricane in January 1941.

I replied: '*Open the hood first*, trim her hands off at 130 mph, undo your straps, pull out your intercom plug and roll on your back.'

Then came the final call 'OK Griff, I've got the hood open, straps undone, plug coming out...'

Then silence, which seemed to last for hours. Would he be able to keep the nose up if he rolled too slowly with no rudder to help when the aircraft was on its side? How would the Spitfire behave after he left it? And where would it land?

Here Tom Stewart joined in the drama. It was extraordinary how fate constantly threw Old Mac, Stewart and me together in our aeronautical evolutions.

He called 'I've been listening to the drama. I'm in an Oxford, just north of Cheltenham – can I assist?'

I replied 'His bearing from us was 195° magnetic on his last transmission. You could look for a parachute floating down on that bearing.'

Tom acknowledged. We waited in the hushed tower. Bad news always spreads quickly and all aircraft airborne having overheard the drama kept silent.

Thoughts rushed through my head. Curiously such faith had I in our parachute packers it never occurred to me that his parachute wouldn't open! My concern was where the now-short-of-fuel Spitfire was going to land and would anyone be killed.

The phone rang; stridently it seemed. 'Royal Observer Corps here; I have to report that a V_2 has landed in a field adjoining the Gloucester – Worcester – Cheltenham Road junction at Coombe Hill. Maybe it was meant for your airfield.'

Although the V_2 bombardment of London had commenced none had landed far away from the London area. This V_2 was Mac's Spitfire on its way down!

Now commenced an operation which, had it been planned, would never have worked.

I called Tom and told him where the Spitfire had crashed. He replied 'I'm nearly at Coombe Hill. I'm flying up that reciprocal bearing you gave me. I'll fly downwind from Coombe Hill and see if I can see anything.'

We waited in the silence of the control room hoping that Tom Stewart might catch sight of a parachute floating down. The cloud base was only about 2000 feet, so Mac would have an eerie descent through 7000 feet of cloud before he would emerge at the bottom with another 2000 feet to go.

Then came an excited call from Tom, 'I can see the Group Captain gathering up his parachute in a ploughed field right alongside the Smiths Instrument Factory airfield near Bishop's Cleeve. I'll land and pick him up.'

A quick phone call to Smiths Instruments to tell them what was going on and ten minutes later Tom called up. 'Am airborne from Smith's. Have got the Group Captain. He's unhurt. His trousers are covered in mud. He's got his chute and even the ripcord handle. Be with you in ten minutes.'

Another quick phone call to the Mess and a clean uniform was sent down from Mac's room to his office. Tom taxied over the grass right up to the Headquarters and afterwards Mac used to say that it only took him 25 minutes from baling out at 9000 feet to sitting in his Office chair again!

And the Spitfire? I think it is still there; in a field but about 20 feet below the surface south west of the junction of the A4019 with the A38 at Coombe Hill. No wonder the

Observer Corps thought it was a V_2. The ground was soft when it embedded itself in the field at full terminal velocity. Only the wings and tailplane were on the surface so we collected the bits, smoothed over the top of the hole it had made and left it to the archeologists of the future. And the reason why the rudder had come off? A sad story for if orders are obeyed, technical work in the Royal Air Force is practically foolproof. In this instance one man was fitting the new rudder and had almost finished but had not inserted the locking wires into the nuts when he was taken off the job and put on to something else more urgent. The next day someone else was detailed to finish the work and didn't spot that the locking wires were not all in position but he signed up the work as being completed and so did his NCO (for in the RAF it is mandatory that one man always checks another man's work). A sad story but at least Mac survived.

During the spring and early summer of 1945 we experienced more aerial dramas.

I have always subscribed to the view that from the moment they are born aircraft are determined to destroy themselves. Ships also have this inclination but to a lesser degree. The reason why aircraft are so affected is that they are creatures of the air and they are unhappy on the ground where, curiously, they spend the major part of their lives. Unlike a bird, when at rest, they cannot fold their wings and are therefore a prey to every breeze that blows and every mechanically propelled vehicle which comes close to them. They are also vulnerable in the air, not only to each other but if there is a way of colliding with the ground in an abnormal attitude, an aeroplane will think up how to do it. And the Boeing was no exception to this propensity.

It may be some solace to the modern air traveller that this proclivity in the behaviour of aircraft is slowly becoming less. This is due to their greater size and weight, for gales on the ground don't effect them today nearly as much as their predecessors of yore – the fabric covered biplanes.

Perhaps the aircraft are not entirely to blame for being accident prone. Having on occasions been given the task of investigating accidents with a view to 'allocating blame and making recommendations to prevent a recurrence', as the usual instruction details, I am convinced that the Lord sits in his heaven and notes a unit which is getting slack or perhaps over confident. He then decides that there shall be an accident to teach them a lesson. Sometimes it takes Him several weeks to arrange an accident for being so aware of the ease with which aircraft try to injure themselves, all ground personnel and aircrews are constantly on their guard. So some accidents take two or three months longer.

In the case of the Boeing the Lord had His plans completed by 9th April 1945. On this glorious spring day with a light easterly wind I took off for a final airtest of the automatic homing and landing equipment. My crew consisted of Figaro Barber and Flight Sergeant Dolbear, who was a highly qualified electrician and who had not only installed the Minneapolis Honeywell electric autopilot in the aircraft but 'found' enough power for the electrics by installing a 'chore horse' petrol engine driving a generator in the toilet compartment, exhausting through a hole cut in the side. Modern Air Inspection Board Inspectors would have had a fit but during the war temporary arrangements such as this were acceptable – at a research unit.

All went well as we cruised round the Vale of Evesham admiring the blossoming apple trees. It was one of those days when you felt embarrassed to be paid for doing such a pleasant job as flying.

She was homing herself back to the airfield prior to coming in to land on the automatics. I selected wheels down for the undercarriage and when it was half-way down it jammed!

I took control from the autopilot and cruised around still unconcerned. We'd had problems like this before. But this time there was no sorting it out; Figaro and Dolbear tried to get the wheels right down using the emergency manual system. Nothing happened. It was jammed solid, in the half-way down position.

Thoughts went racing through my mind, especially the thought of Mac's Scottish wrath if I broke the Boeing. If I could land her with the undercarriage half down and if the propellers didn't strike the ground and if she didn't go on her nose we could still save the day for the demonstration on the morrow. There were a lot of 'ifs'.

And tomorrow's demonstration was of the greatest importance as Mac had emphasised. It was to show George Gardner, Head of a Department at RAE Farnborough, just what the Boeing could do. We expected him to be critical of our ideas for we had already proved that Moseley's system had to be used with an electric autopilot and Gardner had designed the remarkable 'huff and puff' Mk VIII autopilot which had nobly guided our Lancasters, Halifaxes and Wellingtons throughout the war. It was a compressed air autopilot and although it worked to a degree it was nowhere near accurate enough for our purpose. Obviously the designer of the Mk VIII autopilot wouldn't like to be told that his baby wasn't up to the job.

But landing in our present condition had to be faced. Knowing that the centre of gravity on landing would be too far forward it meant that the Boeing was likely to go up on her nose. I sent Figaro and Dolbear to sit in the lavatory on top of the now quiet chore horse engine in the hope of keeping her tail down. The tower was already fully aware of our condition and had confirmed what I could just see myself from the crew compartment: that the wheels were only partly down.

To obtain the lowest landing speed possible I decided to land dead into wind on the grass. Having experienced 'burn ups' caused by sparks igniting leaking fuel or hydraulic lines on runway 'undercarriage up' landings I chose the grass to eliminate any fire risk if things went seriously wrong. This was in the days before the fire fighters had devised the

Submarine H33. The flat section (the folded fore plane) about 20 feet from the bow made an excellent platform on which to embark and disembark from the Walrus. With the submarine stopped, the technique was to taxi the Walrus in at right angles. Matelots with brooms would fend the aircraft off while crew were transferred. The Walrus would then be let out on a 30 fathom line, and would ride windrode without fear of damage

Some of the crew of Submarine H 33 in 'pirate dress': Lieut Chapman, W Armishaw, DSM (Coxswain) and Lieut TD Wood, DSC. *Photo: RN Submarine Museum, HMS Dolphin, Gosport*

modern method of laying a foam carpet on the runway to kill the sparks and fire risk.

Although I say so myself, it was a perfect approach and an oh so gentle landing on the exact spot I wanted. I had switched off both engines and made a glide approach. The starboard engine stopped in the right position with the twin bladed propeller horizontal. For some reason the port propeller was still windmilling. We were only doing about ten miles an hour after a gentle touchdown when up she went on her nose.

One of the best things about aviation is that, unlike the sea, there is no tradition about the Captain leaving the ship last. I'd already experienced two good prangs; one a burn up. I was first out closely followed by Figaro and Dolbear. I dashed to the front to estimate the damage. It didn't look too bad. Just the nose crushed in a bit. Then I noticed a clod of earth on the tip of the port propeller. If the plumbers (engineers) saw that it would mean an engine change. If a propeller ever struck the ground or any object it was a golden rule that the engine must be changed in case internal damage had occurred. I knew it hadn't – the ground was very soft – so I quickly knocked the clod off the propeller tip and polished it with my handkerchief rotating it until it was horizontal like the starboard prop! Then with my foot I pressed flat a few divots cut up by the spinning prop and awaited the arrival of the plumbers.

Easing the tail down we could see there was no damage except to the broken in nose. This nose had been specially made in America of a new material called 'plastic' to house an experimental radar scanner. There wasn't a hope of obtaining a replacement but by now the Boeing had endeared itself to the hearts of the technical fraternity and they announced; 'She will fly tomorrow with the wheels fixed down; have no fear.'

All through the night work went on, laying up strips of plywood over the broken nose. Each layer had to be glued and

117

dried with hair dryers from the WAAF site before the next layer could be applied. The repair had to satisfy the AIB Inspector and he expected it to withstand a dive of up to 300 miles per hour. Whether the Boeing with its thick wing conformation could ever have attained this speed, even in a vertical dive, is a moot point.

By 0730 hours she was pushed out of the hangar by the bleary eyed maintenance crew. With her undercarriage locked down and reinforced with angle iron straps Figaro, Dolbear and I clambered aboard and took her up to the heavens. When her original Wasp engines had worn themselves out about six months previously, we found that no replacements were available so we had installed two of the noisiest engines ever constructed. These were out of Harvard aircraft. The propellers were ungeared and had only two 'angle of attack' positions, fine and coarse. It was said that in the fine position the tips of the propellers exceeded the speed of sound. The noise the Boeing made with two of these engines was quite extraordinary and distinctive and I gloried in flying over Overbury village in fine pitch where Mac lived and where he would now be masticating his wartime breakfast of reconstituted powdered egg. He recognised the noise and it brought joy to his heart.

And so the demonstration to George Gardner (subsequently Head of RAE) did take place. He came, he flew and he was conquered and in due course, after a further demonstration to the Minister for Civil Aviation, Viscount Swinton, on 25th July 1945, the powers that be agreed to form a special unit known as the Blind Landing Experimental Unit. I was appointed to bring it into being. Figaro Barber was to come with me.

However, before this took place yet another aerial drama occurred.

In the spring of 1945, although the war was drawing to a close, great advances were still being made in the use of radar in aircraft for submarine detection. One of the latest equipments was produced by TRE and fitted to a Warwick aircraft. It had such capabilities that it was reputed to be able to see a Heinz baked bean can floating on a calm sea at three miles.

Whether it really could do this we never really proved because the Warwick decided to commit suicide before we could prove the point.

The Warwick was the largest twin engined aircraft in the RAF at the end of the war. Like its predecessor, the Wellington, of which it was a blown up version, it was geodetically constructed. The Wellington had done sterling work in both Bomber and Coast Commands throughout the war. Its curious construction of aluminium frames covered with canvas could take an extraordinary amount of punishment. Much of the flak directed at Wellington went straight through it and slapping a few patches on the canvas and rivetting in a few new frames would soon have it flying again in no time. Because the 'spiders web' construction was weakened by providing hatches of a decent size the Wellington wasn't the easiest aircraft to get out of in a hurry and the Warwick was little better in this respect.

On 12th May 1945, Warwick No 772 required an engine and airframe test after having this latest radar equipment installed. Information to the radar display was fed by a very large external scanner under the aircraft's belly and this was housed in a streamlined plastic radar dome.

This test merely required the aircraft to be flown after being some time out of commission. I was taking her up solo when Lieutenant Commander Tony Milward asked if he could come with me and have some dual instruction. Although essentially a webfooted single engined pilot in charge of the Naval Section, Tony Milward was very keen to fly everything on the station and as yet the 'Warwick' was not in his list of 'Types Flown'.

I carried out the tests required then we landed and

changed seats. Tony did one circuit and landing then we taxied back and he carried out another take-off. He retracted the undercarriage and we had just reached about 150 feet when there was an enormous explosion on the port side. It was easy to see what had happened. The large single tyre of the port main undercarriage had exploded in its nacelle with such force that it had blown out the rivetted panels immediately above it on top of the wing.

This was rather disconcerting so we changed seats and I took control again.

Tony and I were now victims of a design feature which fortunately was soon to be eradicated by the introduction of the multi wheel main undercarriage whereby the weight of the aircraft on the ground could be taken by several tyres so that if one tyre deflated the results would not be disastrous. However, that time had not yet come and we were airborne on a summer's evening with obviously only one main wheel to land on. Furthermore, there wasn't much wind. With a strong headwind and the slower landing speeds of wartime aircraft it was sometimes possible to land with minimal damage by landing on one wheel and holding the damaged flat tyre off the ground as long as possible. Finally it would have to take the ground and the drag of the damaged tyre would pull you off the runway out of control. Occasionally the severe sideways loading would collapse the undercarriage and it could pierce the fuel tanks and start a fire.

It was soon apparent that we couldn't land on even one wheel as neither of the undercarriage legs would come down.

So be it! It was to be a belly landing! Not all that uncommon in that day and age but it did mean that considerable damage would be done to the aircraft and the beautiful new scanner in its streamlined plastic housing would be obliterated.

It was essential to reduce the aircraft's weight to a minimum before landing, which necessitated using up as much fuel as possible. Luckily there were only about two hours' fuel in the tanks. Flying around Worcestershire and Herefordshire in the calm air of a glorious May evening can be very enjoyable but my enjoyment was inhibited by the certain knowledge that I was about to do a great deal of damage to this lovely new aeroplane.

With the fuel nearly all consumed and darkness coming on we prepared ourselves for the landing. Tony removed the escape hatch over my head and then strapped himself into the wireless operator's seat with the lap-strap and waited for me to tell him over the intercom when to lie forward on the table cushioning his head on his folded arms which was the recommended position for crash landings.

I had already decided to land on the grass rather than risk sparks by landing on the runway. We came in nicely over the hedge; I told Tony to brace himself for the deceleration, knocked all electrical and ignition switches off and waited for the crunch.

When it came the deceleration was startling. I had expected it to be much smoother. So great was it that the Elsan was torn from its floor mountings in the tail of the aircraft and shot past my right ear to flatten itself on the instrument panel.

Again, as there is no tradition in the RAF about the Captain leaving last, I was out first quickly followed by Tony. We found ourselves being sprayed by petrol and ran from the aircraft with our feet and trousers soaked in high octane fuel. Unknown to us there were 500 gallons of high octane fuel still in the bomb bay tanks and these had been most effectively punctured by the radar scanner!

It was fortunate that I had chosen the grass to land on rather than the runway! The slightest spark would have caused a burn-up and this would have affected the future of civil aviation, for Tony Milward was to have a most successful post war career as Chairman of British European Airways.

And why hadn't I known that the bomb bay tanks were

fitted and were full to the brim? My own fault entirely. The aircraft's Form 700 gave full details of the fuel state and the capacity of each tank. I had glanced at it merely noting that there was plenty of fuel for our half hour flight. In the air it was not possible to tell that the bomb bay tanks were full as they were not provided with fuel gauges.

I really didn't deserve to get away with this oversight. And the reason the tyre burst? It was never established. Tyres still do it even today. Presumably we must accept that they are entitled to burst occasionally.

The scientific successes which we achieved were not only due to the scientists themselves but the manner in which the uniformed personnel treated them. It would have been disastrous had they been put into uniform. Constrained, they would never have flourished, but left to themselves with the minimum of constriction they flourished like weeds.

Their courage and coolness during aviation 'incidents' were a recurring surprise to the aircrews. These attributes may have been due to their intense concentration on the task in hand coupled with their lack of flying experience.

A certain Boffin Roose (not his real name) fulfilled this category. He lived in the Officers' Mess at Defford and rumour had it that he only possessed one suit of clothes, slept in his underwear and had never been known to take a bath. An officer remarked one day that 'Boffin Roose doesn't even dry himself properly. He has soap behind his ears.' This remark was countered by the reply: 'well thank the Lord he has soap behind his ears. At least it proves he washes even if he doesn't take a bath.'

But Roose was popular despite his lack of conformity, slovenly dress, unruly hair and complete ignorance of service traditions. He was not averse to frequenting the bar where he imbibed somewhat liberally.

One of his projects in temporary form was installed in a Wellington, which because of its 'lattice' construction, had rather small emergency exits; small because it was necessary to preserve the strength of the structure. Normal exit and entry was made from underneath just in front of the co-pilot's position but this larger point of egress was not available in the event of a belly landing.

On the day when Roose was to achieve fame the wind was from the west and for take-off it was necessary for the aircraft to use the short runway. This runway was bounded by a ridge at the upwind end some fifty feet high. This ridge separated the airfield from the park of Lady Coventry's magnificent country house at Croome D'Abitot.

A power failure just as the aircraft was airborne with wheels retracting ensured that it struck the top of the ridge and slithered to a stop on its belly in the middle of the park with one engine on fire.

The crew evacuated the aircraft rapidly popping out of the top hatches like rabbits. Being experienced they ran a good distance from the aircraft for aircrews of that era had plenty of experience of crashed aircraft and post-crash small fires, which could erupt into a monstrous 'woof' as the fuel tanks blew up. Distance ensured the retention of a decent complexion.

But there was no sign of Boffin Roose. He must be stuck inside the aircraft somewhere and yet the wheels up landing had not been severe. None of the RAF crew had suffered an injury so why should Boffin Roose not have evacuated the aircraft as quickly as they had. Surely he had more sense than to try and get out through the normal entry door in the belly?

They moved back towards the aircraft all fearing the 'woof' and sheet of flame. Then a figure appeared in the hatchway above the pilot's seat clutching a 'breadboard' of electronics. It was Boffin Roose who, realising that his equipment was about to be incinerated, had gone back into the burning aircraft to rescue it. He was lucky to be only superficially singed.

After 48 hours in sick quarters he appeared in the mess

again wearing borrowed clothes, for it was confirmed that indeed he only had one suit. Roose was a hero and, we all thought, so was the officer who lent him the clothes for he would never want them returned!

But this devotion to the task in hand was normal boffin behaviour. My experiences with them led me to understand in the post war period why some of them defected to Russia. Politics didn't interest them. The war was over. They were loyal to their own country while there was a war on but as soon as it was finished their loyalty was to their own research and the country which offered them the best research facilities got them.

This opinion may be contentious but if accepted it does help to mitigate to a degree the apparent disloyalty of the defectors.

CHAPTER 8

The birth of BLEU

'You know when you are landing crosswind and you start pushing the rudder pedals from side to side and stirring the porridge with the control column, you are wasting your time. My anemometer readings on the ground show clearly that you need 'X' degrees of aileron or 'Y' degrees of rudder and the aircraft should land smoothly. I know that you can do a smooth crosswind landing using your method but why on earth do you 'stir the porridge' so much? Its not really necessary you know'. So spoke the boffin.

BLEU (Blind Landing Experimental Unit) had been formed in September 1945 at RAF Martlesham Heath under the aegis of RAE Farnborough, and the great wartime 'crash strip' of Woodbridge had been placed at our disposal for practical flying trials.

All Mac's plotting and cunning had come to fruition and basic research had started on what was finally to culminate some 33 years later in automatic landings being accepted for both civil and military aviation. But there was a long way to go. For instance we, the British, still had no electric auto pilot, nor a suitable civil aircraft with a tricycle undercarriage.

Despite the lessons which we should have learnt from the Americans only Handley Page was producing an aircraft with a tricycle undercarriage: the Hermes. All the other manufacturers were still designing to the conventional (sit up and beg) undercarriage. Tricycle undercarriages were essential for future automatic landings.

The original Boeing demonstrations with Moseley's black box and a Minneapolis Honeywell Autopilot had caused a flutter among the scientists. While the Boeing could do adequate but somewhat heavy automatic landings the scientists wanted to know why, so at BLEU we had to get down to some basic research and find out.

Volunteers had been called for from the Research Establishments at Farnborough and Malvern and curiously nearly all these volunteers were young and sailing enthusiasts. The list read like Widecombe Fair; Tom Pearson, Colwyn Stone, Chalky White, Dave Burgess, 'Scrim' Scrimshaw. Although civilians, all of them had gained considerable flying experience during the war, on occasions being quickly clad in a uniform and sent off to work some new piece of equipment on operations. They were just the men for the new unit and their enthusiasm for sailing which is, in many ways, so akin to flying stood them in good stead.

Martlesham Heath had been a research establishment before the war and had excellent accommodation and laboratories but the airfield itself was small, hence the choice of Woodbridge crash strip for our practical flying.

There was however an aura of melancholy at Woodbridge occasioned by a monument to the efforts of the Royal Air Force and the United States Air Force during the war. It consisted of some four acres of crashed, broken and shot-up aircraft piled on top of each other to a height of about thirty feet – relics of the sharp end of the Air Forces which had fought, suffered and managed to get back home. Each fuselage could tell its own story of human endeavour and engineers' ingenuity to get it back across the cold North Sea, some landing with crews still aboard and some badly crippled landing with pilots only or pilots and engineers only aboard, the remainder of the crews having baled out.

I once entered the scrap dump to search for spare parts for one of our aircraft. I found the parts I wanted but I found other things which told their tale. Bloodstained helmets, discarded field dressings, empty hypodermic capsules and the dross of aerial battle. No stone memorial could engender the same appreciation of the courage, the suffering and the price paid by the aircrews, as this monument of scrap aluminium soon to be melted down into saucepans.

But I was disturbed to have my crosswind landings criticised.

The aircraft used to determine how we did crosswind landings was a twin-engined Oxford. Not the easiest aircraft to fly. Although it was a training aircraft it had all the inherent faults of aeroplanes built into it which was as it should be for it is better to break a cheap aircraft in training than a very expensive operational one later, which would happen if pilots were trained on docile machines.

This particular aircraft had 'desyns' fitted to the controls and these could record every movement the pilot made. Hence the boffins remarks about stirring the porridge.

I must admit the print-out showed an awful lot of reciprocal movement just before touch-down so I tried making crosswind landings according to the boffins' calculations, with frightening results.

Then we tried crosswind landings with the Boeing on automatics. It made my heart sing to see the Boeing, untouched by hand, 'stirring the porridge with much oscillation of rudder pedals' just as I did manually! Moseley's black box knew what to do even if we didn't know why! Later we were to prove, as we pilots knew already, that as we approached the ground the windspeed varied considerably in strength and sometimes in direction during the last twenty feet hence the porridge stirring to compensate.

That is merely an example of what went on at BLEU and although it took 33 years to get the system in service it certainly was thoroughly tested and tried – tried to such an extent that every part or portion of the system is triple covered for failure and today, as I thunder into London Heathrow as a passenger in thick fog with the aircraft on automatics, I have complete confidence in the system and merely envy the pilots the 'intensity lighting' at the runway threshold which was not available in our original trials.

Although the Boeing 247D had been the means of bringing us as a nation into the forefront of Autolanding it was finally handed back to TRE at Defford. This may have been pique on the part of our new masters, RAE Farnborough, who maybe did not like this 'evidence' of another establishment's accomplishment, for hell hath nothing to compare with the jealousy of one scientific establishment for another where research is concerned.

But this Boeing, RAF No DZ 203, proved to me that aeroplanes had souls. We had flown together on and off for nearly five years and she went back to Defford, in my opinion heartbroken. She was parked in a hangar which during the war had been erected for camouflage purposes close to oak trees. One night a mighty Worcestershire oak blew down, smashed through the hangar roof and broke the Boeing's back. That was the end of the Boeing.

I sometimes wonder if the Americans are aware of the great contribution made to the war effort by this docile slow aircraft for it flew the first 10 centimetre radar which gave our night fighters a breakthrough, helped enormously in the research into submarine detection and finally gave us the political and financial muscle to produce our own auto-landing system. Verily this was one piece of 'lease-lend' that paid substantial dividends.

But the time had come for Figaro Barber and me to go to pastures new. Figaro to be an entrepreneur in civilian life where he applied much of the knowledge he had gained in the designing, manufacturing and marketing of the 'Pinta' Automatic Pilot for small sea-going craft while I was sent off to the Royal Canadian Air Force Staff College at Armour Heights, Toronto to learn to 'fly a mahogany bomber' (RAF parlance for a pilot engaged in administrative duties).

CHAPTER 9

Ferio Ferendo

It was an hour before a hushed tropical dawn at Negombo, Ceylon on the 9th November 1946. We pored over the charts in the Met Office.

'I just don't know what's going on between here, Sabang and Singapore,' said the Forecaster. 'If aircraft flew the route daily I'd be able to give you a forecast but it's now two days since an aircraft flew either way and I have no actuals to go on. What you're looking at is a chart three days old. The ITF (Intertropical Front) is there all right but how far north or south of its old position and how active it is I just don't know.

'A 51 Squadron York tried to get through yesterday but they returned when they found the ADF (Automatic Direction Finding) compass unserviceable. They are having a shot at getting through today and have just gone out to their aircraft. The sooner you get to the Malacca Straits the less build-up there will be.'

It was just over seven years since my last dash to Singapore in a twin engined Blenheim. It looked as though this trip was going to be similar only this time I was a passenger in a York transport aircraft, MW 295, with four engines, approaching from Ceylon. Last time I had flown down from Calcutta but it looked as though, once again, the Malacca Straits were going to give us a worrying time.

I was now a Staff Officer with 47 Group, the long range

Group of Transport Command and the Air Officer Commanding thought that it would be a good introduction to my new appointment as 'Wing Commander Operations' to get out onto the routes as a passenger and experience what went on.

So far it hadn't been a bad trip flying with a passenger qualified crew captained by a New Zealander called 'Joe' Lennon. All the crew were efficient, hardened by the maul of war. The only difficulty was interpreting their different dialects. Lennon was easy to understand despite poor intercom with 4000 horsepower roaring on the wings, but the Wireless Operator, Flight Lieutenant Brenner, was very Scottish, the second pilot Flying Officer Good, and the Air Quatermaster, Sergeant Kelly, were from Southern Ireland, while the navigator Lomas was Lancastrian. Only the Flight Engineer, Steel, spoke English. Verily it was a babel of tongues forward of the crew compartment bulkhead.

Apart from the noise our only discomfort was caused by a surfeit of eggs. While I seldom saw an egg in a shell during the war there now seemed to be a plethora of them. This was now the fifth day after leaving Lyneham in Wiltshire and we had eggs for breakfast each day, egg sandwiches or hard boiled eggs for an airborne lunch and egg and chips on landing at Malta, Habbaniya (Iraq), Mauripur (Karachi) and Negombo (Ceylon). Thus we must have each eaten at least 21 eggs already since leaving England.

As we landed at each staging post our handling by ground personnel varied. Not unnaturally the war being over and the majority of personnel being conscripts their thoughts were centred on when they would be demobilised and a conversation with the most uncommunicative individual could be started merely be asking him for his demob group number. It was noticeable that in the more remote staging posts the morale was sky high, especially if there weren't any women there but as always the more fleshpots available the lower the esprit de corps.

In its early days Transport Command did not enjoy a very good name. Aircrews who could fly nightly on raids from England to Berlin found it a very different story to fly from England to Singapore. The hazards of sandstorms, the inter-tropical front (ITF) and the lack of navigational aids after the magnificent coverage over Europe afforded by 'Gee' proved greater than the hazards of German opposition. Other Commands of the Service, with the RAF flair for hyperbole, gave the embryo Command in those early days the slogan 'From VIP to RIP in three flights'.

The man who knocked it into shape and made it the fine Command it eventually became was Air Chief Marshal The Hon Sir Ralph A Cochrane. Under his direction it was brought to unexpected standards of training and safety and proved the truth of its official motto, Ferio ferendo ('I strike by carrying' or more freely 'Transport is my weapon') in the supreme test of the Berlin Airlift in 1948 and 1949.

But as I was to discover we hadn't reached that stage of efficiency – yet.

The Commander in Chief had introduced a training system which graded crews into categories 'A' and 'B' (allowed to carry VIPs), 'C' (passenger qualified) and 'D' (freight only). Furthermore, any passenger sitting in an aircraft knew that the crew flying him was not only passenger qualified but had carried out their 'continuation training' within 28 days of the journey they were now undertaking. 'Cont Training' as it was called consisted of several hours practising emergency drills; two engined and three engined landings, fire drills, ditching drills, etc. It cost a lot of money to find the training hours to do this for there were no simulators in those days but for a passenger it was comforting to sit in the back and know that within the previous 28 days the crew flying the aircraft had been thoroughly tested in all emergencies.

Flt Lt Lennon's crew were 'B' Category which just as well for we met the ITF some two hours before we reached Sabang, the turning point at the top of Sumatra. Turning the corner was going to be a problem because Sabang itself is 2,000 feet high and the mainland hills to the south are 7000 feet. Our forward visibility was only three to four hundred yards and the rainclouds pressed us down to only four hundred feet above the sea on the radio altimeter.

I was sitting in the second pilot's seat at this stage and, on the off chance of a reply, I called up on the radio the 51 Squadron aircraft MOYAB that had taken off ahead of us and got an immediate reply. He was half an hour ahead of us at 14,500 feet fighting his way through the intertropical front and was going higher to try and get over the top.

In the event he didn't make Singapore. Quite correctly he dared not come down inside the ITF not being sure of his position and next day we learnt that he turned North to fly out of the ITF and he made a successful landing on an ex-Japanese landing strip at Port Blair in the Andaman Islands. The strip was too small for the York to fly out from, so the passengers had to be ferried to Rangoon in Dakotas and it was two months before the strip could be repaired and lengthened so that we could recover our York aircraft.

Such was Transport Flying in the immediate post war period.

Our own situation deteriorated as we approached Sabang and we all experienced deep concern. There was a Medium Frequency beacon at Sabang but Flt Lt Brenner, while he could receive it, could not sense it. With the Estimated Time of Arrival at the corner only five minutes away Lennon changed course North East in the hope that we'd miss it in the driving rain. Luckily the rain ceased temporarily and there, over to starboard where it should be and bang on our ETA was the island of Pulo Wei. I recognised it from my previous association with this part of the world in 1939. Lomas's navigation couldn't be faulted. We soon picked up Diamant Point and flew at little more than 150 feet all the way to Singapore.

I thought this part of the trip was going to be as bad as my previous arrival by Blenheim in the ITF of 1939 but this time we had three extra aids; a radio altimeter, an accurate map showing the islands (and some were shaped like sauce bottles towering to 600 feet) and we knew where we were, having made our departure from Diamant Point. At this low altitude with hardly any forward visibility our greatest problem was to navigate between two islands 15 miles apart and each one 600 feet high. We felt fairly confident on this point and so long as we didn't hit a ship's mast we should get through.

And get through we did, touching down on the pierced steel planking of the Japanese constructed airstrip of Changi seven hours and thirty minutes from Ceylon. Then we sat down to a welcome meal in the Transit Mess of Egg and Chips - my 15th egg in 5 days!

The total flying time England-Singapore was 38 hours and 20 minutes. Seven years previously it had taken me 44 hours and 25 minutes in a Blenheim.

There was still a post war atmosphere about Singapore. A few Japanese POW working parties were employed on the landing strip which the Japanese had made on soft ground at Changi Creek. Eventually it became a major international airport but meanwhile everything was very temporary including the Transit Mess. Temporary latrines were being constructed behind the Mess where a Chinese carpenter was cutting out the lavatory seats by placing his topee on the square top to the thunder boxes, scribing a line round the brim of his topee and then cutting out the hole with a padsaw! So that's how they determined the shape!

I flew back with Lennon's crew as far as Karachi and to avoid the bad weather build-up in the Malacca Straits which gets worse as the day goes on we left early and flew straight over Sumatra and direct to Negombo with the ITF on our starboard side most of the way. Then on to Karachi where I left Lennon's crew to fly with some Category 'D' (non-passenger qualified) crews for a change.

The first crew I flew with impressed me enormously. The Captain was a Flt Lt 'Jock' Campbell. We flew with a load of freight from Mauripur to Palam (Delhi) and then back again. If this was the quality of the 'D' category crews I felt the Command had little to worry about the crews being trained for passenger carrying. Although I was the only passenger Campbell showed me the safety exits tactfully remarking that they varied with different aircraft. On the flight Campbell navigated to Delhi while his co-pilot flew on instruments for practice and the navigator as co-pilot/look out. When I asked Campbell if he'd been able to receive any beacons, he had not only received them all: Karachi, Jodhpur and Palam, but listed their ranges. Not only was every radio facility used despite the excellent weather but he took sextant shots for practice. At Palam, Campbell ensured that all four propellers were lined up with one blade vertical to the ground.

This was 'Captaincy'. I was so impressed on this flight with Campbell and his crew that, curiously, as it will be seen, it became a turning point in my life.

On arrival back at Mauripur being anxious to get back towards the United Kingdom I jumped on to another York aircraft flown by a 'D' Category crew which was just leaving for Shaibah near Basra, Southern Iraq.

It was to be a night flight and I sank into my seat in the freight compartment glad to close my eyes and relax, little realising that apart from war experiences this was to be almost the worst flight of my life.

Nothing wakens up a pilot quicker than a change of engine note. The inner starboard engine was giving off a continuous sheet of flame from the inboard exhaust ports. The engine was soon feathered.

Nothing to worry about. We still had three engines and we must have reduced our weight considerably as it was $5\frac{1}{2}$ hours since we had taken off.

I visited the crew compartment and immediately sensed an

air of concern and a 'loss of confidence'.

The navigator's chart didn't impress me. Our track was marked but no positions or bearings on it. He reckoned we were about one hour from Shaibah. We were now flying North up the Persian Gulf.

I went back to my seat.

On our ETA I had hoped to see the lights of Basra. No lights appeared and then I realised that the moon had changed sides. We must be flying South.

Another visit to the crew compartment did nothing to raise my morale. We were now down to 3,500 feet. Neither the pilot on vhf (voice) could raise Shaibah nor the radio operator on 333 kcs. Yet we must be somewhere near our destination. Then the flames from an oil refinery appeared ahead of us. Which was it, Abadan in Persia or Kuwait?

At this point the navigator shot through to the freight compartment and searched frantically in his baggage, finally emerging with the Air Almanac on the front of which was a picture of some ancient mariner carrying a quarterstaff and underneath the picture the inscription 'Man is not lost'.

He was going to try and get a position line from the moon with his sextant. I feared that even if he could work the sight out properly the low altitude of the moon and the aircraft rolling about on three engines did not promise an accurate result.

We'd now been airborne almost seven hours. There were still three hours to dawn and we had 700 gallons left; enough for about 3 hours. Meanwhile the wireless operator had raised Almaza in Egypt, Castel Benito in Libya and Habbaniya west of Baghdad.

Then the propeller of the inner port engine started to run away in fine pitch.

I could see us ending up in the Persian Gulf or the desert or, if we wandered over to the East at this altitude, we might leave our bones in the Zagros Mountains of Persia.

I looked in the cupboard behind the Wireless Operator for

the life-saving jackets. The cupboard was bare! In the freight compartment I had seen some parachutes. I checked them. There were sufficient for us all but on examining the escape hatch a frame to carry radio compass equipment had been installed over the top and it couldn't be opened. The only way out was to lower the ladder from the roof of the freight compartment and go out through a hatch on top which would undoubtedly ensure that anyone making a parachute jump from that exit would tangle with the tail plane.

The prospects were not promising.

Going back to the crew compartment to report my findings a different atmosphere prevailed. The Wireless Operator had obtained a Class I bearing to fly on to reach Shaibah. At last Shaibah had answered but how far away were we and would the engines last out? If the flaming oil refinery we had been flying over was Abadan, we still had 100 miles to go.

We limped along and at last the flashing beacon of Shaibah showed up and we were able to talk to the tower.

A night landing on 2½ engines could be risky. Always in fear of a burn-up and a jammed door I looked for the axe. It wasn't in its holder by the door. Then I remembered that the Air Quartermaster had been opening tins of condensed milk with it for our coffee. I retrieved it.

I may have looked undignified but I sat strapped in my lone seat in the freight hold waiting for the landing with the sticky axe across my knees.

There was an agonising half minute as we screamed our way in 'over the hedge' after a slight undershoot but when it came it was a good landing.

As we walked over to the Reception Centre I noticed the RAF Ensign still flying in the moonlight on the flagstaff. Ensigns flying at night, propellers 'matched' on the ground; both mere symbols but they do indicate a standard of efficiency.

And the reason why we couldn't raise Shaibah for

bearings: a ground wireless operator asleep when on duty who failed to hear our calls for help. Luckily RAF Habbaniya had heard us and got on to Shaibah by landline. We had been too low and too far away for the pilot's transmissions on vhf to be heard. A sad story.

The York MW 163 in which I had flown from Mauripur was going to be delayed for an engine change and a propeller change so I arranged to fly the next leg to Almaza near Cairo in MW 205 which was also being flown by a Category 'D' crew.

Then occurred the incident that affected the rest of my life. My baggage was loaded on to MW 205 and while carrying out the departure clearance with the crew I noticed a signal giving the ETA of Flt Lt Campbell who was homeward bound in MW 188. The incident the night before in MW 163 had sapped my morale and having been so impressed with Jock Campbell on the Delhi trip I decided to delay and fly with him. I had my bags unloaded from MW 205 and she took off not to be heard of again for two weeks. All the crew were killed when they flew into the hills above Ain Sukna on the west bank of the Gulf of Suez. Yet another case of 'if only they had been ten feet higher'. Nomad Arabs finally found the remains of the aircraft with the load and the crews 'baggage', which also consisted of carpets and tea, spread around the crash site. Thank goodness I saw the signal announcing Jock Campbell's ETA at Shaibah!

After this trip I took up my appointment running 47 Group Operations Room much the wiser.

Apart from ordinary route services throughout the still intact Empire there was the occasional 'flap' on, moving the Parachute Brigade to some strategic point. We had plans for practically every eventuality, the majority of which never happened, but it brought home to me the power of the Command and the truth in our motto 'I strike by carrying'. In the turbulent post-war world many a minor conflagration became still-born by merely moving a parachute battalion to the nearest British possession.

The Transport Force had taken the place of the Battleship of old.

One thing did become evident on these minor operations. I began to understand why Nelson's Captains were able to deduce what Nelson intended or indeed where he had gone to without any form of signal intelligence. It was because 'They knew his mind'. Thus some Captain would sail out to the Mediterranean to join him and not finding him would say to himself 'Ah – obviously he has gone to the West Indies' so off he'd go to the West Indies, thousands of miles away, and there he would find Nelson.

It was the same with our Transport Operations. The need to keep radio silence meant that we could not issue changes of plans and orders to our aircraft Captains once the operation had started. Yet time and again Captains anticipated instructions, sorted out their own difficulties when aircraft went unserviceable at remote outposts. Merely issuing the 'aim of the operation' to Captains before it began enabled them to use their own judgement and carry out operations quicker and with greater facility than the finest planning staff could devise.

Not that all was serene and quiet in our Operations Room. Indeed the Ops Room was always bedlam throughout the 24 hours, whether there was a 'flap' on or not.

Indeed we eventually selected a motto taken from Kipling's 'If' which we displayed on the wall. It read:-

> If you can keep your head
>   When all about you
> Are losing theirs and blaming it on you,
>   You don't understand the situation.

CHAPTER 10

'Jumbo'

Came the Berlin Airlift which was the crucible in which the Command's Training System was proved, for by this time very high standards had been achieved.

The Airlift also solved a mystery which had puzzled the Germans for some time.

One advantage which the Allies possessed over the Germans was a sense of humour and, in the shadowy world of scientific invention, this paid off handsomely during the 1939/45 war for we gave the most bizarre names to our inventions which provided no inkling as to their purpose; names such as Monica, Mandrel, Gee, H_2S, Rebecca, Eureka, Serrate.

On both sides there was a constant effort to discover what radio or radar device the opposition would next produce.

We were lucky because our nonsensical titles enabled us to hide their purpose in their initial development and their early operational use. The Germans, on the other hand, through their choice of names helped us to determine their purpose quite quickly. For example the German device 'Freya' we quickly determined was a radar detection system for 'Freya' was a Nordic goddess who possessed a necklace which was guarded by a minor deity 'who could see 100 miles'. It did not take long for our sleuths to find by photographic reconnaissance and through resistance friends the Freya detection stations which were evenly spaced out 'like the pearls on a necklace'.

Another German device was called 'Wotan'. Our classically educated boffins knew that Wotan was another god who had only one eye and in due course deduced that Wotan provided a bombing system which comprised only one beam and a distance measuring device which could be used to determine a dropping point for bombing purposes. Their previous system 'Knickebein' needed two beams to determine a bombing point. This one-eyed idiosyncrasy gave the game away.

So the war went on with the Allies generally a jump ahead and the scientific intelligence personnel trying to discover what the other side was doing.

But there was one device developed by the British which the Germans never deduced, during the war. I believe it is also true to state that its secret was so well kept that only a few of the scientists who flew from RAF Defford and TRE crews knew of its use and potential. It would be safe to say that even our own scientific super sleuth Dr R V Jones*, who knew most things, was unaware of 'Jumbo', for that was its name.

Curiously the story of how the secrets of 'Jumbo' were finally revealed to the Germans starts well before the war when a German youth called Dollman was sent to stay with a family in Norfolk to improve his English; in fact he spent several summer vacations with this family in Norfolk and became such an anglophile and countryman that he took to wearing 'plus-fours'.

Came the war and Dollman, called up for military service, failed his medical; but because of his excellent English he was appointed as a civilian interpreter in the German equivalent of our Scientific Intelligence.

His war was spent making translations of recorded conversations intercepted from airborne aircraft and be-

---

* Author of 'Most Secret War'

tween prisoners of war at interrogation centres. Both sides had advanced listening devices and one especial source the Germans had was the four engined Condor flights which flew, as required, from airfields in the area of Brest to Northern Norway and vice versa, round the west of Ireland keeping judiciously out of range of our landbased fighters. While the primary reason for these flights was meteorological and reconnaissance, listening to our airborne transmissions was a further bonus.

The Germans had heard conversations from TRE identified aircraft in which the subject matter was 'Jumbo'. The first time these transmissions were heard was in 1942 and transmissions about 'Jumbo' continued until the end of the war but despite all the efforts of their Scientific Intelligence services and interrogation of aircrew prisoners the Germans were unable to gain intelligence as to what threat 'Jumbo' portrayed in detail.

The general opinion in Germany was that 'Jumbo' was a new navigational device, though no intelligence revealed the frequency on which it operated. Conversations had been intercepted from aircraft to a ground station but the ground station could rarely be heard. They were of this nature:-

Aircraft:- When do you expect Jumbo to switch off?

Aircraft:- Is Jumbo out of bed yet?

Ground Station:- Not properly. The blankets are up to his chin.

Aircraft:- I have Jumbo at 30 miles.

Ground Station:- Jumbo will be on all night.

That it was TRE aircraft which made these transmissions was especially worrying to the Germans for it was this Establishment which had perfected such accurate bombing aids as Oboe and H_2S. Their desire to discover the operational use of Jumbo was a top priority.

The war went on and finally finished and no one was interested as to what Jumbo would have achieved! Even Dollman who had been translating these curious messages forgot about Jumbo.

Times were hard in Germany after the cessation of hostilities but Dollman managed to obtain employment as an interpreter on an RAF airfield in Germany dealing with the employment of civilian labour.

Came the Berlin Airlift and Dollman was employed in the Air Movements Section at Wunsdorf in a responsible position dealing with the civilian labour loading the York aircraft with bagged coal destined for Berlin.

He had a pleasant personality, a certain 'presence' and soon got to know the York aircrew – indeed such was the quality of his accent and manner of dress that he was often taken for an Englishman.

Now it came to pass that among the York crew was a pilot called Pat who had, for two years, commanded a four engined research flight flying for TRE from RAF Defford near Worcester. He was a mature batchelor and now a senior transport captain holding the highest flying qualifications. He had three loves – his flying, his pipe and his pint.

One evening Pat and some of his brother officers visited a biergarten on the far side of the Steinhudermeer from Wunsdorf and there he got into conversation with Dollman. Dollman remarked that he was amazed how the York crews were able to operate in such appalling weather conditions and the conversation ranged over the subject of radar aids. Dollman pricked up his ears when Pat mentioned that he had flown on radar research for TRE at Defford during the war.

The RAF officers remarked on Dollman's precise knowledge of our radar aids and Dollman then told them of his job during the war translating intercepted messages for his scientific intelligence chiefs.

Then right out of the blue he said to Pat 'Did you ever work on "Jumbo"?' Pat, who was quaffing a stein of beer at

143

the time, suddenly spluttered and said 'Did you say Jumbo? What on earth do you know about "Jumbo"?'

'Not much' replied Dollman 'but we guessed it was probably a navigational aid something like "Gee".' Pat put down his stein of beer alongside his beloved pipe and chuckling rubbed his hands together between his knees; a habit he had when he was highly amused. 'I think' he chuckled, 'I can tell you about Jumbo without infringing the Official Secrets Act. It wasn't a radar device – it was a mountain! Well, not exactly a mountain but a well known landmark known as the Hill of Bredon not far from our airfield at Defford, and we held it in great awe because mini-mountains close to the circuit of an airfield and aeroplanes don't mix very well.'

'By calling the Hill of Bredon "Jumbo" we could ask Air Traffic Control about the weather conditions without revealing anything to you Germans. For instance "Jumbo" isn't out of bed yet but he has his head out of the blankets" meant that there was fog or low cloud obscuring the lower slopes in the Vale of Evesham.'

CHAPTER 11

French Gravity

He was a small wiry man, slightly gingery in looks and temperament. At a race meeting he would have been taken for an experienced jockey. I was in awe of him but he must have been a nice man for he had a dog, a Sealyham called 'Binks' who worshipped him and men who are loved by dogs are usually nice men.

His name was Sergeant Forster. A flying instructor at No. 3 Flying Training School, Grantham and although our love/hate relationship was to last for only three months it marked me for the rest of my life. He was a hard man but his teaching enabled me to live to a ripe old age for it saved my life on several occasions.

There is a poster seen on the walls of some American Flying Training Schools which shows an aircraft stranded in the top of a tree and below it is written this axiom:-

Aviation in itself is not inherently dangerous.
But to an even greater degree than the sea it
is terribly unforgiving of any carelessness,
incapacity or neglect.

I realise the truth of this now. I didn't in 1936 for I was a very keen, thoroughly overconfident pupil and must have been a pain in the neck to Sgt Forster.

It may seem strange to the other services but although I was a commissioned officer and Forster was a Sergeant I called him 'Sir' - in the air. This was normal RAF practice and rightly so.

RAF initial flying training is tougher than in civil aviation for a pupil is introduced earlier to such practices as 'recovery from unusual positions' and aerobatics. It soon sorts out those who may kill themselves through slow reactions and those who suffer from airsickness. I was one of the latter. Forster knew that overconfidence and airsickness were my chief problems and he set out to eradicate them.

The cure for overconfidence was fairly painless. Coming in for my last solo landing in a Hart biplane on a Friday afternoon I had a little drift on and should have gone round again. My port wing tip grazed the ground, happily without damage. I thought no one had seen me but Forster had. On entering the office to sign the authorisation book as having completed my detail he said: 'why didn't you go round again when you made that ghastly landing? You will report to the hangar at 0800 hours tomorrow morning and wash four aircraft, Sir.' (We were now on the ground where our seniority was reversed.)

Next day was Saturday when I had a weekend off and had intended going to London. I found myself washing aircraft with hot water and soap getting all the grease and mire off. Engines in 1936 had a habit of spraying oil in the slipstream. I can smell the smell of the soap to this day but the punishment helped to curb my overconfidence.

Curing my airsickness was a more difficult problem. It first manifested itself doing steep turns. On announcing to Sgt Forster that I was about to be sick he said 'OK I've got her - you be sick over the port side'. Whereupon he put the Hart into a steep turn then came out and flew straight and level while I threw my heart up. Then we would do a milder exercise while I recovered and then back to the steep turns.

I learnt a lot while overcoming this airsickness problem.

His remark about being sick over the port side was born of long experience of pupils being sick in the seat in front of him. Such was the rotation of the propeller that in a Hart aircraft the slipstream assisted disposal on the port side, but had a ghastly result if the pupil 'threw up' on the starboard side. In any case there was a certain amount of washing down to be done on landing but this was by no means an unusual occurrence amongst the pupils.

Plastic bags had not been invented in 1936 nor had waterproof airsickness bags but I evolved a system which solved my problem. I obtained strong brown paper bags from the kitchens. Although they weren't waterproof and their used 'life' was limited they lasted sufficiently long enough to be thrown over the side (the *port* side) over the sparsely populated Lincolnshire countryside and then we would carry on with the lesson. Another trick I evolved was to read the manuals assiduously. I would then concentrate on getting near perfect results first time so that the exercise would not be prolonged and I could escape before nausea set in!

But Sgt Forster was thorough, however unpleasant the manoeuvre we had to achieve. As a change from 'recovery from unusual positions' and aerobatics we would do forced landing practice which, in the days of biplanes, had not changed since the 1914-18 war.

The drill was to select a field on engine failure, keep plenty of height in hand and do a series of 'S' turns on the downwind side of the selected field then make the final approach in a sideslip.

Sideslipping more or less went out with the introduction of monoplanes though there are some old bold pilots of quite large monoplanes who have got themselves out of a difficulty using this old fashioned technique.

Briefly it is a means of losing height rapidly without stalling the aircraft and was an excellent way of getting into a small field over high trees etc without too much excess speed. By putting on full rudder and opposite stick the aircraft

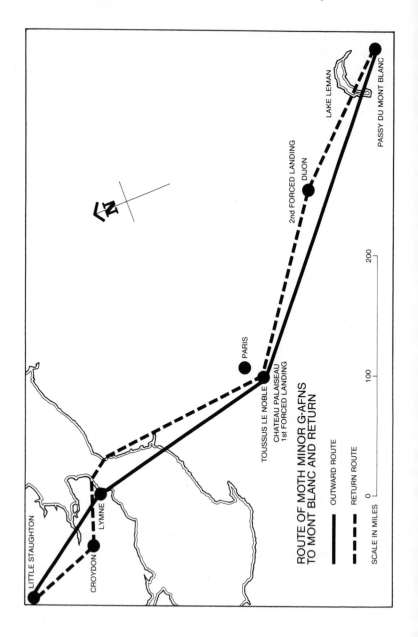

ROUTE OF MOTH MINOR G-AFNS
TO MONT BLANC AND RETURN

OUTWARD ROUTE
RETURN ROUTE

SCALE IN MILES
0   100   200

LITTLE STAUGHTON

CROYDON

LYMNE

TOUSSUS LE NOBLE
CHATEAU PALAISEAU
1st FORCED LANDING

PARIS

2nd FORCED LANDING
DIJON

LAKE LEMAN

PASSY DU MONT BLANC

would yaw violently with its nose up and appear to fall out of control to the ground. In fact it still had flying speed and by releasing all pressures and centring all controls just before hitting the ground a superb 'spot' landing could result with the minimum of 'float' or landing roll.

Sgt Forster made me practise sideslipping and forced landings for hour after hour. I loved doing them. He was a biplane pilot of the old school himself. Carrying out real forced landings had been part of his life and he was determined to see that I could do them.

Yet aircraft reliability was improving in the 1930s and eleven years were to go by before I had any occasion to put this part of his teaching into practice.

In August 1947 my 14-year-old brother-in-law David required to go to friends in France for his summer holidays to learn French. I thought it would be fun to hire a civil aircraft from the RAF Flying Club and fly him out to an airfield then known as Passy du Mont Blanc, St Gervais, which was right under the massif of the Mont Blanc near Chamonix. The trip was especially appealing as it would give me some practical flying; a change to get away from the perpetual panics of the operations room.

I selected a Moth Minor for the flight. This aircraft was intended to be the replacement aircraft for the beloved and world renowned Tiger Moth. It was a monoplane with two open cockpits and an endurance of about five hours. This gave a range of over 500 miles in still air.

The Saturday morning found us airborne from Little Staughton in Bedfordshire heading for Lympne to clear customs. Anticyclonic weather was forecast but it was a hard push to Lympne against the strong south-easterly headwind and we only managed a ground speed of 60 mph. At Lympne we donned our Mae West lifejackets for the channel crossing and all went well as far as Paris where the wind had dropped to calm and the temperature had risen to the eighties fahrenheit. I cleared customs at Le Toussus Airport, refuelled and completed formalities then taxied out with every hope of reaching Passy du Mont Blanc before dark.

Alas it was not to be! I had run up the engine, checked magnetos and was about to line up for take-off when the engine stopped dead. Pumping the throttle failed to 'catch the prop'. I thought I must have inadvertently knocked off the switches so sudden was the engine's demise. For the next forty five minutes I swung the propeller forwards, backwards, with switches on and with switches off and with the throttle set at all points of its range. Nothing happened. Sometimes the engine would cough and that was all.

Some years previously I had flown a Magister which was occasionally temperamental when starting and I would lift its tail in the air and shake it; then it would go. I tried this trick finally on the Moth Minor and behold, she started! I ran her up again. All was correct except for the slight shock when I touched the port magneto switch. We took off and set course for Dijon.

I had just settled down to cruising revs at a height of 2000 feet when the engine stopped dead. It was discouraging. Down below was a ribbon developed suburb of Paris. Had we been a mile either side of our present position we should have been in open country.

As we glided down I did all the things Sgt Forster had taught me, such as checking petrol tanks, switches etc. It was no use. The engine refused to pick up. I told the boy David that the engine had packed up and that I would try and land in the field down below us. He replied, quite nonchalantly, 'OK'. It was his first flight and he seemed to think that this was normal aviation routine. The field I had picked, the only field in fact, was the park of a Château. On three sides it was surrounded by high trees and on the approach side by quite the highest high tension cables in Europe. I did the usual 'S' turns as drilled into me by Sgt Forster, and then the crucial moment arrived. The Moth Minor is a monoplane and not suitable for side-slipping but this one did – it just had to. We slipped nicely over the cables but arrived at deck level with 70 miles per hour on the clock instead of the fifty I had wanted. I carried the sideslip over the ground. Over half the field had been used up before we touched down amongst some tree stumps and rocks. It was downhill and ahead of us was a herd of Friesian cattle. We stopped just twenty yards short of the first cow and about 100 yards short of the far hedge.

I experienced a great feeling of satisfaction at having executed a forced landing successfully; at least the aeroplane was the right way up, which was more than I had hoped. However I had heard a loud bang as we touched down amongst the tree stumps and on jumping out I found the tail wheel flat. It was most fortunate that the main wheels seemed to have missed everything.

It is a strange thing that Englishmen abroad like wearing the weirdest clothes! Clothes which at home they would not be seen dead or alive in. Perhaps our customs and climate force us to dress dully and dolefully at home with the result that when we do go to someone else's country we cast off our inhibitions and sally forth in the most wondrous garments. On this occasion I was wearing a red shirt. It was a Scottish tartan type. I had bought it in Canada and had brought it back to the United Kingdom intending to wear it at home but at the last moment my courage had failed me. It was only on my trips to the continent that I was able to wear this shirt surreptitiously. I was on my knees examining the burst tail wheel when I felt hot breath down my neck. The herd of cows were now surrounding the aircraft and were showing more than an ordinary interest in my shirt. At least I wasn't too sure whether it was the aeroplane or my shirt but I needn't have worried for one minute we were surrounded by twenty cows and the next it was 200 people and the cows had been elbowed out to the back row of the scrum.

Everyone spoke at once. In my broken French I explained what had happened and then I lifted up the cowling to see if the engine was still there. It was a fatal move. I went down in the ensuing rush and came out behind the scrum like a badly trampled scrum half. Fortunately there was a man amongst the crowd shaped like a gorilla with three days growth of beard. He held the crowd back and breathed down my neck while I looked at the engine. The carburettor was full of petrol and so were the fuel filters. All the plug leads were on. Without any tools I couldn't check much further.

I asked the gorilla where the nearest phone was and he offered to take me to his house. I left the boy David in charge of the aircraft with instructions to keep the natives out of the cockpit and to endeavour to stop them tearing the rest of the aircraft apart while I was away phoning the airport.

As we were walking to his house the gorilla told me that the field in which I had landed was the grounds of a priests' seminary known as the Château Palaiseau. We skirted the walls of this château as we climbed up the sides of the valley to his house.

Now the French telephone system in 1947 was unique. It was difficult for a Frenchman to get any results on a French telephone and for an Englishman it was practically impossible. Although I was only eight miles away from the aerodrome at Le Toussus and although the instrument had an earpiece for each ear I could hardly hear and spent about two minutes shouting 'Alo,' 'Alo,' 'Alo.' I could do this part very well, so well in fact that the person on the other end thought that I was French and replied at about 400 words per minute. I had to speak very slowly and explain that I was English and only spoke French 'un petit peu'.

After a while I got the necessary information across and they informed me that they would send out an 'engineer'. The gorilla and I drank a bottle of beer apiece and then set off back to the aircraft.

It was hot, desperately hot. This August Bank Holiday weekend in England broke all records for heat and in France it was no different – only hotter. As we walked back I realised the amazing luck we had had in finding anywhere to land. The aircraft was in a field in what might have been the bottom of the Cheddar Gorge. At the approach end of the field there was a huge viaduct which fortunately the Germans had blown up thus facilitating my final approach. All around there were houses, trees and high tension cables and amongst it all this oasis of sanctuary.

There seemed to be an even greater crowd around the aircraft on our return. The original throng had been supplemented by some boy scouts and some priests from the adjoining seminary.

The heat and the beer made me feel like lying under a tree and going to sleep but I was eager to get the aircraft pushed back to the approach end of the field where it would be more accessible to the engineer when he arrived and also in a position from which I could take-off should we succeed in getting the engine to perform satisfactorily. While the crowd was present it would be a good opportunity to get the aircraft moved. As the tail wheel was flat it would be necessary to carry the tail to prevent further damage to the tyre and inner tube. I had learnt over the phone that there was little hope of getting the tyre repaired either in situ or at Le Toussus, should I ever get back there. There was apparently a shortage of tyre solution in France. I would therefore have to carry on flying with a flat tailwheel. Tailskids were in vogue before tailwheels and the flat tyre could act as a tailskid just so long as I could get the aeroplane back to England in one piece.

Before moving the aircraft I had one more try at starting her. I went through all the correct drill but even waving the tail in the air failed to get her started. One of the priests asked me why we shook the tail about. I answered 'superstition' (the only appropriate French word I could think of on the spur of the moment). He looked at me in a most peculiar manner and didn't seem to be able to make up his mind whether I was just rude or mad.

There was no lack of volunteers when it came to pushing back the aircraft to the other end of the field. I put the gorilla and another heavy man on top of the engine to weigh down the nose so that the tail was easily lifted by three people. The rest of the crowd pushed on the mainplane. We averaged about 6 knots across the field and it took me all my time to steer the tail in order to make the main wheels miss the tree stumps, rocks and molehills. I began to feel very dubious about the take-off.

After getting the aircraft into a reasonable position for take-off we unloaded her. I had decided that if the engine performed well enough I should leave the boy David behind with the luggage and that I should take-off solo in the hope of getting out of the field and back to Le Toussus aerodrome where I could pick him up again. As we made a pile of our luggage on the ground so the crowd kept picking things up and examining them. Mae Wests would be picked up and passed round the crowd with as much noise and gesticulation as that employed by Irishmen examining poultry at a fair. While endeavouring to retrieve one thing another would be picked up and passed round. The small boys and priests were equally bad. Appeals to the senior priest, a man of great rotundity, had little effect and I found myself beginning to condone the deeds of Henry VIII and King Herod.

Finally I retrieved all our belongings and lay under the shade of a tree while things quietened down. The crowd also relaxed and sat in the shade. The priests stood around the wings and periodically drummed their fingers on the fabric. The great heat, the buzzing of the bees, and the inane nattering of the natives were sending me to sleep. Suddenly the priests stiffened. The talking ceased and I could sense an indefinable something in the air. Then I saw what it was. Bearing down on us from the far end of the field was a simply enormous priest. It was the Father Superior of the seminary. Apparently in this particular order seniority was in order of weight. He gave an order to the rotund one who in turn spoke

154

to the other priests and they all withdrew to the seminary. It was not good that they should show interest in things so mundane. I rejoiced to see them waddling wearily away in order of weight.

Soon after the departure of the priests the engineer arrived together with a taxi driver and an English speaking French girl. By a strange coincidence I knew the girl quite well for I had had a contretemps with her on a former occasion when passing through Le Toussus. She had relieved me of 300 francs which I had presumed were for landing charges. Later I noticed that her receipt was a plain one. On my return journey through Le Toussus I asked her what the charges were for and she informed me that she had no official position at the airport as I had supposed but that she had charged me 300 francs for showing me round the various offices! She had found it difficult finding suitable employment after the war and had appointed herself unofficial liaison officer to visiting pilots! She now worked for a French aircraft firm at Le Toussus.

I explained the symptoms of my engine failure to the engineer and my suspicions about the port mag switch which emitted a slight shock when I touched it. He proceeded to check the contact breakers, plugs, switches etc. He was biased against the magneto right from the start. It was a 'drole' magneto he said, for it was really two in one with one armature and two contact breakers. Quite an unusual design and rarely found in aero engines.

While he tinkered with the engine I set off on foot to check over the field for take-off. It was 570 paces long – ample for my requirements but there were some tall poplar trees about 200 yards beyond the far hedge and there was also a clump of trees in the middle of the field. This clump and the various tree stumps and rocks necessitated a curved run on take-off. I wasn't very worried about this as it takes me all my time to keep an aircraft straight on take-off anyway. A nice half circle to the left would be more suited to my natural habits. The field was uphill for the first half – so much so that it was impossible to see the far end. However, on top of the ridge grew a large thistle and by leaving this thistle some four feet to starboard of the propeller I should pass between tree stumps in its vicinity and then get a bead on the tallest poplar the far end. It wasn't an ideal take-off run but with the aircraft lightened and the engine going properly I thought it should work out all right.

By the time I returned to the aircraft the engineer had carried out a thorough examination of the ignition system and fuel filters. All the time he kept shaking his head for he couldn't find anything wrong. It was Saturday and nearly five o'clock, French time. He put everything together again. We swung the propeller and the engine started. It gave 2200 revs on run up. I was satisfied but the engineer wasn't. He was worried for he had found nothing wrong. However he suggested that I should take-off and fly to Le Toussus where he would give the engine another thorough check over on the morrow.

I climbed into the cockpit, waved away the stones which were acting as chocks, got the tail up on the brakes and let her go straight for the big thistle. I had thought that all the crowd were at the take-off end of the field. Little did I realise that half of them were out of sight over the brow of the hill on their way to the far end of the field to see me pile up. As I breasted the brow of the hill near the thistle there was the crowd in front of me but not for long. Some ran and some just lay on the ground. I missed them all and cleared the poplar trees easily. I climbed up to 3000 feet above the field just in case the engine stopped again and then set course back to Le Toussus.

I arrived safely then realised that I must face up to a financial crisis. British currency restrictions had resulted in my having only 2000 francs on me and I should have to pay the firm who sent the engineer, the taximan who brought him out to the field and finally our hotel for the night. Fortunately the taximan only charged me 800 francs (about £1.55p). But I felt bound to disclose my financial position to the aviation firm 'Escadrille Mercure'. Mademoiselle, to whom I confided my financial situation, arranged matters so that I could pay on my way back from Chamonix where I knew I could borrow some money and meanwhile she said she could fix us up with a cheap hotel for the night. We could also travel on the firms transport to Versailles which would not cost us anything.

We pushed the Moth into the hangar for the night and set off for Versailles. On the way into Paris the bus kept stopping at taverns for the workmen to slake their thirsts. It was a pleasant trip and life had taken on a rosier hue by the time we debussed at Versailles. Mademoiselle escorted us to a cheap hotel; so cheap that it cost us only 180 francs (37p) for the two of us, payable in advance! The fact that I didn't sleep very much for fear of having our throats cut during the night shows just how cheap an hotel it was. There was a dance hall next to our room and when I was awake I suffered from the heat, the music and the drunken brawls; when I slept I dreamt of high tension cables, broken viaducts and priests.

Next morning, which was a Sunday, we travelled out to the airport on the workmen's bus again. On the way we stopped at a low tavern and breakfasted on fried eggs washed down with lashings of hot coffee and hot rolls.

At this cafe I saw the heaviest man in all France. The engineers thought that he was the heaviest in the world for he weighed 215 kilos (30 odd stone). His amorphous body oozed out of the kitchen carrying a chair. He waddled out of the café to a seat in front where he sat down 'fore and aft' for the chair he was carrying had been brought to support his stomach. He spent all his days sitting outside the café with his stomach on the chair and his hands folded over the back of it. Poor chap.

I liked the fitters of Escadrille Mercure even though it did take them a long time to get to work and to get home. They gave the Moth Minor a thorough going over but found nothing wrong. This puzzled them for on the first run up she ran very badly and then recovered. To give them their due they admitted that they could find nothing wrong, apart from the intermittent shorting of one magneto switch. At noon David and I were airborne again for Passy du Mont Blanc; a 3½ hour hop.

The weather was still perfect so I climbed up to 7000 feet and stayed there. The journey was uneventful until we were over Lake Geneva when the engine once more stopped dead. I had plenty of height in hand and could easily have glided to Geneva Airport some three miles away on my starboard hand. I still suspected the magneto switch leads so I undid the button which holds the instrument panel in place and pulled the whole thing out towards me. I gave the switch wires a good shake and slammed the panel back into position, and on looking up I found we were in a steep climb and quickly pushed the stick forward which gave us a negative 'G' loading, whereupon the engine restarted! Had I but realised it this restarting on negative 'G' loading should have indicated to me the cause of my engine failures but, at the time, I missed this clue.

I considered for a while the feasibility of landing at Geneva but had I done so I should have been in a difficult situation having no Swiss money. I therefore decided to press on to Passy keeping as high as possible. I knew of two really big fields, ex aerodromes, where I could get down if I had to at Annemasse and Bonneville. I felt I would rather force land in French territory where I had friends and could get money rather than land in Switzerland where I should have neither.

The next thirty miles up the valley to Passy were worrying. Although I kept at 6000 feet the mountains towered up to the right and left of me and ahead Mont Blanc glinted in the sun at nearly 15,000 feet. Annemasse went by and then Bonneville went by. I had either to reach Passy now or land in the bottom of the valley. Luckily it turned out to be Passy. I kept our height until we were right over the aerodrome and then cut the throttle whereupon the engine stopped.

I couldn't have cared less – if I broke the aeroplane now at least I should be among friends. Fortunately we came to rest in the middle of the aerodrome. Sgt Forster would have been proud of my 'S' turns, sideslipping and landing.

It was so hot that we could hear the dried grass complaining. We just left everything and walked over to the house where I knew the aerodrome owner lived. Not a living thing stirred. Everyone was having a siesta overcome by the great heat. Soon we were lying back in the shade drinking copious draughts of wine mixed with water while I poured out my troubles to Monsieur Guiron.

Monsieur Guiron was an old Maquisard and whom I knew well. He had been a pilot in the 1914/18 war and in the 'tween war years had set up a very successful business at Passy du Mont Blanc flying tourists round the summit of the mountain and on occasions landing on the mountain on skis. He was also a qualified aeronautical engineer and was now re-establishing his tourist business.

He cross-examined me closely and then announced most definitely that my trouble was petrol. He upbraided me for not seeing my own tanks filled at Paris and threw both hands in the air when I said I had not got a chamois leather with me to use for filtering purposes. Although M Guiron is a great patriot he said 'Never trust a Frenchman filling up an aeroplane – all Frenchmen today are rogues – you English are too trusting!' etc. etc. 'We will drink wine until it is cool, then we shall tow your plane in with my car and look into things.'

After a further half hour's wine drinking and a long discussion on Communism we set off to tow in the Moth. M Guiron had everything buttoned. He made a rope bridle fast to the aircraft oleos and towed her with his car, prop first, while the boy David and I carried the tailplane to save what was left of the tailwheel tyre.

On arrival at the hangar we examined the reservoirs under the petrol pumps. Both were full of dirt and at Paris they had been quite clean. On removing the hollow bolt which holds the petrol feed pipe on to the carburettor M Guiron cried 'Voila! Here is no filter. There should be one.' I was inclined to agree with him and yet surely the petrol pump filters above the reservoirs should have been sufficient to stop any dirt reaching the carburettor. M Guiron announced that he would soon find a filter and armed with an adjustable spanner he went into a nearby scrap dump. He removed the petrol unions on a couple of Renaults and announced that someone had been there first. Finally he found just what he wanted on a Citroen and proceeded to remove a slieve filter.

We returned to the Moth and the filter fitted perfectly. The next job we tackled was the tail wheel. On dismantling we found that the outer cover was badly cut in two places and that the valve had pulled out of the inner tube. It was rather an unusual valve fitting for it was bent at right angles in order to come out of the side of the wheel. As the original valve had been vulcanised in the tube and as we couldn't repeat the operation we had to get a French bicycle tyre valve with a screw compression type base and adapt it to suit. This meant a very delicate brazing operation. At Paris at one of the premier airports of France they had been unable to do the job!

Having delivered the boy David I had intended setting off back to England the next day. At dawn I was awakened by a peal of thunder and realised that I was shut in by a typical Alpine storm. Flying weather in the Alps generally is much better than most people imagine. There is never any doubtful flying weather for it is either perfect or impossible. And it was quite impossible on this day for the valley was filled all day with lightning, thunder, lashing rain storms and low cloud. It cleared towards evening but too late to start for England, or even Paris. I fitted the repaired tail wheel and carried out an air test instead.

I was still unhappy about the engine for as I explained to M Guiron we had fitted a filter but there still might be dirt between the new filter and the jets. I wanted to dismantle the carburettor but Guiron advised against it as he considered the carburettor was 'trop compliqué' and we might not be able to get it together again properly. It certainly did look complicated so I took his advice.

The engine started perfectly and I flew round for ten minutes. She behaved well on all throttle settings and it was a joy to land and taxi in on an inflated tailwheel again. I felt much happier about the return trip now for I only had the weather to worry about. That's what I thought.

Next day was perfect and I set off for Dijon flying as high as possible just in case. This time the engine ran perfectly but another worry manifested itself soon after crossing the Jura mountains as both petrol gauges read Zero! When I had set off from Passy I reckoned that I had eight gallons left, four in each tank, but the gauges dropped rapidly from the 3 mark to zero. I kept flying for ten minutes a time on each tank so that when one tank finally cut I should know exactly how many more minutes I might get out of the other before the engine would finally stop. The last half hour to Dijon was agony. Although the terrain was getting better for an 'atterisage forcé' the gauges reading zero seemed to mesmerise me and my mouth was dry the whole time. Far better to have a complete engine cut without warning than to suffer this agony. At last Dijon aerodrome hove in sight. I maintained my height until I was within easy engineless gliding distance.

When I had landed I had flown five hours since the last refuelling. I had estimated that the Moth's endurance with 26 gallons aboard might be 6 hours but either faulty petrol gauges or too much full power climbing to 8000 feet after each take-off had reduced this.

After refuelling I taxied out but had great difficulty in keeping the engine going. She would only run at half throttle or more and I taxied along making a noise like a flying boat picking up moorings on the blipping motor method. I ran up on the brakes before take-off. Everything was correct at full throttle. Of course I shouldn't have taken off. I should have gone back to the hangars and torn the engine apart until I found something wrong but when you are running late on schedule and you are hot and harassed and short of money in a foreign country the correct action doesn't always appeal.

Anyway I took off and climbed on track towards Paris. The land rose rapidly with me as I climbed over the escarpment at the west side of the Rhône valley. Ahead of me as far as the eye could see was the great Forest of Pasques. I hesitated about flying over it for I had not as yet climbed more than 3000 feet. It was a lucky premonition that made me turn slightly to port and follow a tract of treeless country. I had just climbed to 5000 feet when the engine stopped! I almost felt relieved. Subconsciously I had been expecting it ever since I left Passy. I made up my mind that if I managed to pull off this forced-landing I shouldn't get airborne again until I really found the trouble.

I tried all the usual tricks to get her started again but the engine remained quite dead. I had plenty of time in which to choose a field for landing although the ground underneath me was fairly high up itself (about 1000 feet). There seemed so many suitable fields that I even weighed up the pros and cons of choosing a small field near a village where there would be communications, food, accommodation and possibly a garage, or choosing a large long field in an open part of the country. I decided on the latter after considering the principle that no one minds how long you are delayed with an aeroplane so long as you don't break it. If I landed near the village I might just do that.

As I glided lower I found my confidence evaporating for the country on closer examination was extremely hilly, almost mountainous. The field I had selected was on the top of a hill. It was a cornfield half of which had been cut. I first noticed a binder going round and then noticed some high tension cables on the up-wind side. In order to miss the uncut corn, the binder, the sheaves and the cables I had to land crosswind in a narrow strip between two rows of sheaves which ran parallel to the H.T. cables. Sgt Forster in his training had never set me a task such as this. But it turned out all right and even Sgt Forster, stickler as he was, couldn't have criticised my approach and landing. As I rolled to a stop I overtook the binder on my left. An old peasant was driving the two horses pulling it. He looked at me as though aeroplanes landing beside him in a field were an everyday occurrence. He just continued on his crosswind leg, completed his circuit and only stopped when he came round to me next time. I explained to him that 'my motor was dead' and asked him where I might borrow some tools. He gave me all the tools which he had in a box on the binder then he mounted to his rostrum and just carried on cutting corn.

What tools they were! Seemingly it is the habit of all farmers in all countries to possess tools which are completely worn out with maltreatment and useless. However, as I got to work on the engine I felt an amazing contentment creeping over me. Here there were no milling crowds. It was cool in the fresh breeze at that altitude and I could 'think'. What a contrast to the forced landing at Palaiseau.

With the aid of the old man's worn out screwdriver I removed the cowling and decided that the carburettor had to come to pieces. It was the only thing which had not been dismantled so far and I felt sure now that the jets were blocked. Unfortunately the binder tools were completely useless for getting at the carburettor. I was trying to remove the small screws that hold the face plate on the side of the float chamber when a man on a motor cycle arrived. He had something to do with the corn cutting operation and his motor cycle was the most decrepit looking piece of machinery. However he produced from it a wonderful kit of American aircraft tools consisting of chrome vanadium spanners, screwdrivers, pliers and the like. I expressed my amazement and he informed me that he had bought the tool kit from an American Sergeant in 1945. I'm sure the tool kit was worth more than the motor cycle.

With this tool kit I soon had the faceplate off the float chamber and then I could see my trouble. My cry of 'Voilà' sounded most fluent and natural. In the float chamber there were a considerable number of pieces of dirt which by their texture and colour I recognised as being bits of the jointing compound which had been used for making the faceplate tight. This had hardened and broken off in small crystals. I felt sure that some of these bits must have got through as far as the jets but I couldn't find the jets. An aeroplane carburettor is the most complicated affair and I was about to set to and dismantle the whole thing when a girl appeared on a horse. She was about eighteen and very beautiful. After a short stumbling conversation which I had with her in French, it transpired that she spoke fluent English. She lent me her mirror. Only a Frenchwoman would carry a mirror when riding, luckily for me! With the mirror I was able to see behind the carb and so found the jets. I soon had them out and found that, as I had suspected, they were full of the same crystals which were present in the float chamber. I felt greatly relieved for now I had really got down to the trouble and knew that I should get back to the UK. Aeroplanes are really very reliable things and there is no reason why they shouldn't fly properly when there is nothing wrong with them. So I reasoned and as I reasoned my morale rose higher.

I reassembled all the bits and pieces and then realised that I had no locking wire. Again the motor cyclist came to my rescue by removing some of the baling wire from various parts of his motor cycle. In that day and age it was extraordinary how farmers the world over fixed things with baling wire. Baling wire – the universal agricultural panacea! The wire itself was not very suitable for the job and after I'd finished threading it through the various nuts it looked rather like a cat's cradle. Still no one would be able to see it from the ground when I was airborne.

I was just cowling up when a lady doctor arrived somewhat

The Paratechnicon lands successfully (note burst airbags so designed to give 'soft touchdown'). On this occasion it was loaded with a Jeep and trailer, but it could have held 30 soldiers! Luckily this idea of dropping men was superseded by the arrival of the helicopter

Wing Commander Roland Winfield, a doctor at the RAF Institute of Aviation, Farnborough, looking a little anxious while being readied to be snatched off the ground by an Anson—a first

The hook of the Anson has engaged with the highly elastic nylon rope held across two goalposts. Dr Winfield, crouched in the foetal position, can be seen at the foot of the goalposts

A successful snatch! The 'snatchee' can be seen passing the nose of the Halifax while the spectators look on

And away up into the sky goes the 'snatchee' .... Had this project been developed, further means would have evolved for hauling the snatchee into the aircraft, but in this first instance to get back to earth Dr Winfield released himself from his towing harness and descended by parachute. *Photo: Institute of Aviation Medicine*

From Left to Right LAC ATKINSON   F/Sgt SQUIRRELL   Cpl CUSWORTH   LAC SCANLAN
F/O LC BARBER   F/Lt KB HOLLOWELL, AFC   F/Lt J ROGERS   W/C FC GRIFFITHS, DFC AFC
Group Capt JA MacDONALD   F/Sgt DOLBEAR   Sgt BURNINGHAM   F/Sgt ELLIOTT
Cpl POTTER   Cpl HARMAN   LAC REASON   LAC FINCH   Sgt HAYES

The Boeing 247D. RAF No DZ 203. First aircraft known to have executed an automatic landing in the United Kingdom, and the men
who made it possible. Note the ILS aerials and the reverse angle windscreen. Normal on these aircraft, it cut out sunglare and reflection

out of breath. She had seen me land from her villa about 2 miles away and, fearing that I might be injured, she had set off on foot to render first aid. I could not help but compare these highly intellectual and intelligent people with the crowd at Palaiseau. Here there was just the girl with the horse, the lady doctor, the motor cyclist and the old peasant on the binder (the latter still doing his circuits). What a change from the milling priests, small boys and citizens of suburbia at Palaiseau.

When I tested the engine it ran up perfectly. I had no worries about the take-off this time. After saying goodbye to everyone in effusively French fashion I roared into the sky bound for Paris. I felt really happy for a change. All my cares had left me and now I knew that I should get home.

At Le Toussus I taxied up to the hangar occupied by Escadrille Mercure, the firm who had come to my assistance on Saturday. The engineer was surprised to see that I had a blown up tail wheel and he was happy to hear that I had solved my engine problems. His bill, which I now paid, was most reasonable.

Clearing with the authorities at Le Toussus was simple. I was now so well known that I could shake hands with the customs officer and his confederate the security officer and when you reach the stage when you can shake hands with French civil servants you don't have any trouble. I managed to get airborne again in under one hour, the only snag was that I had to clear to Croydon instead of Lympne as the customs at Lympne shut at 4.30 p.m. local time.

Now the direct route from Paris to Croydon crosses a considerable amount of sea and though I felt fairly confident about the reliability of the engine I decided to take the shortest sea crossing from Cap Gris Nez to Dover. When I arrived at Cap Gris Nez the straits were full of shipping and I hardly felt justified in having made the climb to 8000 feet for such a narrow stretch of water.

However distance across water varies with height. In an

aeroplane at 8000 feet the channel seems nothing but from sea level in a Mae West lifejacket your ideas are different. It's just a question of the angle from which you look at it!

CHAPTER 12

Paratechnicon

It was nearly noon local time. Thirty odd thousand feet below us Benbecula bathed in the sunshine of a spring March day. We mushed along in our Boeing 747 now nine hours out from Los Angeles. Ahead of us London Heathrow was offering 500 feet cloudbase and visibility of 1000 yards. Not very good landing conditions but of little consequence in the year 1982 for we should be on automatic approach, with every item of the system three times covered in case of failure of any one part.

I was a passenger in row 40 and yet I was not as safe as I could have been for two reasons. One a habit formed by the public during the 'age of steam' and the other because of our curious laws of customs and excise.

The habit formed in the age of steam was the desire to sit if possible 'facing the engine' and this, in the early propeller days had been accepted by the airline operators as desired by the public. Soon after the 1939/45 war, however, the RAF had seen sense and fitted backward facing passenger seats. With the backward facing passenger seats, in the event of a crash and sudden deceleration, passengers were merely pushed into their seats with their heads and bodies cushioned and supported. With a forward facing seat all they could hope for was at best damaged intestines from the seat belt on a jack-knife and that only if the belt and its anchorages were strong enough to hold the passenger in his seat!

The first RAF transport aircraft to be fitted with backward facing seats were the Hastings and the Valetta. The Hastings was in service for almost twenty-five years and it is said that during that whole time no 'ticketed passenger' was killed. There were inevitably incidents in the tactical (parachuting) role but its record on pure transport work was second to none.

There were crashes of course, two in particular very bad ones, but due to the backward facing seats the passengers escaped entirely.

On 20th December 1950 a Hastings aircraft of 53 Squadron was homeward bound from Singapore and winging its way through a dark North African night laden with 27 passengers and six crew all eagerly looking forward to arriving in the United Kingdom in time for Christmas. As the aircraft droned along over Cyrenaica one of the propeller blades of the starboard inner engine flew off the propeller boss and pierced the fuselage just behind the crew compartment in the area of the rest bunk. Tragically one of the crew members the co-pilot Flight Lieutenant S L Bennett was lying on the rest bunk at the time and was wounded by the propeller blade which not only severed his leg but also the main elevator and rudder control cables. Almost at the same time the now unbalanced engine tore itself from the wing and fell to earth.

Despite this now precarious situation the crew and passengers remained calm. The Captain, Flight Lieutenant Tannadine, managed to keep the aircraft flying despite the of elevator control and the sudden change in the aircraft's centre of gravity due to the loss of an engine. He achieved this by moving the passengers around to regain longitudinal stability coupled with judicious use of the elevator trim tabs and throttles. Another pilot who was aboard, Squadron Leader W G James took over the injured co-pilot's duties and a medical officer who was one of the passengers, Squadron Leader T C Brown, went forward to the restbunk and did what he could for the seriously injured co-pilot, Flight Lieutenant Bennett.

By the exercise of supreme skill and a lot of luck they made a reasonably successful approach to the nearest airfield at Benghasi but, when some 700 yards short of the runway, the Hastings touched down on rough ground, turned over and killed the crew in the crew compartment. All the passengers escaped, their lives being preserved by their backward facing seats, the high backs of which prevented the roof of the inverted aircraft collapsing and crushing them.

The doctor stayed with his patient, the dying co-pilot and as a result of his devotion to duties he sustained serious injuries.

The aircraft's accidents branch and the engineers were desperately anxious to find the engine which had fallen from the wing somewhere over the desert in order to determine why the propeller blade had become detached from the engine. Searches were carried out by air and by vehicle but with no result. Months went by then one day, so the story goes, an astute and observant NCO noticed various, almost new, Hercules engine parts in a scrap merchant's at Tobruk. Thinking that they had been stolen, the Service Police at the local RAF Station at El Adem were informed.

It transpired that the spare parts had been brought in by a Bedouin and sold as scrap. Fortunately the scrap merchant was able to contact his supplier who agreed to lead an RAF recovery party to the place where he had found the engine in the desert. The RAF were only too well aware how quickly scrap metal could disappear in the desert for the Bedouin, after the 1939/45 war, had become expert at dismantling abandoned vehicles, tanks and crashed aircraft which they then sold as scrap. The party hurried on anxious to recover the engine while there was still something left of it. They were lucky for they found the engine nose down in the sand and the essential part which they wanted, the propellor boss, was underneath. The engine was so heavy that the Bedouin had been unable to turn it over and they had run out of the mines with which they usually dug up and used for blowing to pieces the heavier articles they found!

The second incident was at Khartoum. Some 30 Army personnel were returning to the United Kingdom from Singapore. By good fortune the Sergeant in Charge of the Army personnel was a martinet and he briefed his contingent something on these lines:

'Now when you emplane and deplane you will do it in an orderly manner. The front rank will turn right and mount the steps first and take up the seats on the port side. The front rank will be followed by the rear rank who will take up the seats on the starboard side. All will place their small kit on the racks and will wait standing until I give the command "Sit — tighten seat belts".

On deplaning I will give the command "Release seat belts", stand up, collect small kit and remain standing facing inwards. I will then give the order "Port side march out" followed by starboard side. This you will carry out in an orderly manner without any pushing or shoving. You will always take your small kit with you on deplaning. I don't want anything stolen while the aircraft is on the ground.'

The flight proceeded via Negombo, Karachi, Aden and Khartoum and at each staging post the Army passengers were a credit to their service and impressed the RAF personnel. They little realised that their discipline and the Hastings backward facing seats were to save their lives.

At Khartoum Murphy's Law ensured that the civilian refuelling party should fill the Hastings oil tanks with the wrong type of oil. This normally wouldn't have led to a tragedy but in this case it was a detergent oil.

After take off from Khartoum first one engine failed then another and yet another until the aircraft, now returning to the airfield, was flying on only one engine and losing height rapidly. They never did reach the airfield but landed in a timber yard tearing off the wings and fuel tanks and starting an enormous fire. The crew in the front were killed but the main body of the fuselage remained intact and the right way up.

When all movement had ceased the Sergeant stood up and, although a fire was raging, went through his full deplaning regime. All passengers were deplaned without injury and what surprised the Court of Enquiry more than anything was that all soldiers deplaned from the holocaust clutching their small kit!

The other risk to which we passengers in our 747 were exposed was caused by our curious Customs and Excise Laws, for the majority of the 400 passengers were carrying in the passenger cabin with them two bottles of duty free liquor each. One bottle being in the form of highly inflammable whisky or gin. In a crash involving fire this quantity of inflammable spirits (some fifty gallons) would undoubtedly assist in stoking up any fire in the passenger compartment.

But civil airlines still provide forward facing seats because the customer likes to face the way he is going and any simpler system of obtaining 'duty frees' such as buying them before coming through Customs at the place of arrival instead of at the point of departure appears to be beyond the wit of man to devise, so unnecessary risks are still prevalent in civil aviation and one just hopes that no incident will occur whereby it is necessary to evacuate a burning aircraft quickly, soaked in some other passengers' duty free whisky!

Yet another aircraft design feature inherited from the railway age is anachronistic. Why does the toilet compartment have frosted glass in the window? Who is going to look in at thirty odd thousand feet?

In the happy, carefree days of biplanes and propellers, passengers were quite happy to sit in a basket chair screwed to the aircraft floor. If there was a landing incident the aircraft's speed was so slow that the seat problem hardly arose. At

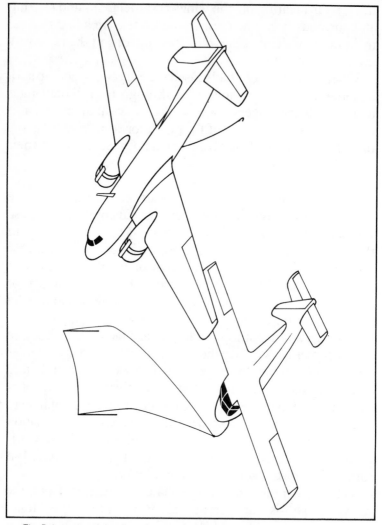

The Dakota aircraft flies at 120 knots some 25 feet above the ground with its 'fishing rod' extended.

When the hook catches the loop of the glider towrope draped over the bamboo 'goalposts' it will be snatched off the fishing rod and draw out tow wire cable from the monster fishing reel inside the aircraft fuselage. This reel is not free running but has a friction brake like an ordinary fishing reel.

Meanwhile the glider accelerates rapidly and the aircraft, now at full throttle and climbing, loses airspeed down to 105 knots then gradually gains speed again with the glider in tow.

172

worst passengers might arrive at the front end of the cabin probably with their seats still attached to them by their lapstraps.

My interest in these matters stems from my appointment, in 1949, to RAF Abingdon to Command the Transport Command Development Unit, where we experimented in conjunction with the Army Airborne Transport and Development Centre, with backward facing seats and other work in connection with Transport problems. Some of the ideas were quite bizarre and many of them were solved by the helicopter which was at last showing promise and about to be introduced to the service.

It is strange that many developments appear to require the provision of an ancillary invention before they can be a success. An example is the steam engine which waited a long time before the invention of mild steel provided a suitable track for the heavy engines to run on. The aeroplane required sophisticated signals equipment and the invention of radar before it could really become a safe means of transport. And in certain fields of military transport work the invention of nylon rope was a necessity in achieving what was achieved by our now obsolete gliders, especially in the field of 'recovery by snatching'.

The early nylon ropes had two great advantages. One was their vastly superior strength over other ropes and the other was their elasticity. This elasticity was especially required to 'pluck' a glider off the ground.

Although the problem is now in the past it says much for human ingenuity that we were able to build a giant fishing reel, four feet in diameter, inside an aircraft on which wire cable was wound culminating in a giant fishing rod suspended below the aircraft.

To recover a glider from a small field from which it was impossible for a powered aircraft to operate all that was required were two bamboo poles some 12 feet high and a length of nylon rope one end of which was attached to the glider and the other led over the poles, called 'goalposts', in the form of a large loop.

When the glider pilot was ready to be recovered a green Very light would be fired and a Dakota aircraft, fitted with internal fishing reel and with its hook extended, would fly over the 'goalposts' and catch the loop of nylon in its hook. There would be a scream from the fishing reel as the cable ran out against its braking mechanism and the nylon rope would be snatched off the goalposts and stretched to almost a third again of its normal length. The glider would then leave the ground with very rapid acceleration. At the same time the Dakota, which aimed to catch the goalposts at 120 knots, would decelerate to about 105 knots. The 'anxiety period' lasted about 5 seconds from the time of snatch. Things could go wrong. Worst of all the Dakota pilot could catch his propellers in the goalpost loop though pilots were so conscious of this danger and the possibility of their own immediate demise this never happened. Perhaps once out of every four attempts the snatch pilot would be too high and his hook would miss the goalposts. This merely led to gasps of irritation by those sitting tensed in the glider waiting to be snatched. Their moment of tension merely had to be endured once more on a second try.

This sytem was further developed for the snatching of men off the ground. This would have been especially useful for agents operating behind the lines and wanting a quick trip home. So far as I know it was never put into practice operationally though one hero who helped to develop the system was snatched off the ground. He was Dr Roland Winfield of RAE Farnborough*.

Recovering gliders which had been used in operations was not the only problem the unit was asked to solve.

Curiously one of the greatest problems in towing gliders was the inability of tug and glider to perform satisfactorily

---

* See 'The Sky Belongs To Them' by Roland Winfield, published by Kimber.

in blind flying conditions. While the glider pilot could see the tow rope and the direction it was leading he could follow the tug and by quick reference to his own blind flying instruments he could at least stay the right way up. Trouble came as soon as the glider pilot was unable to see the tow rope due to thick cloud, darkness or ice on his windscreen. The glider would start paravaning from side to side on the tug and to save himself the tug would cast him off. (Both glider and tug were able to drop the tow should they desire to do so.)

During the war the mass glider landings were carried out in weather which, though often marginal, enabled the glider pilot to see the 'lead' of the tow line. One of the worst glider failures during the war was the two glider attack on the Heavy Water plant in Norway. We attempted to tow them across the North Sea at night. Neither arrived at their planned landing area.

The Development Unit set out to solve this blind flying problem and was reasonably successful in fitting a long arm to the glider, the outward end of which encircled the rope. By a simple mechanical means the movements of the arm (and thus the rope) could be shown on an instrument in the glider pilot's cockpit so that at least the pilot knew in which direction his tug lay.

To test this system, tug and glider would be sent off looking for bad weather. Things looked promising until one day in heavy dark cumulonimbus cloud the glider pilot lost his orientation and cast himself off. He then referred entirely to his own blind flying instruments and descended in a slow, controlled glide hoping that he was not over mountains and praying that if he ever got below cloud level he would find a field to land in.

Imagine his dismay when on breaking out of the cloud he found himself over a large built up area at only 300 feet. There was nowhere to land.

Then he saw a patch of green. A football ground. With

flaps extended he executed a perfect landing to find himself in the middle of Cardiff Arms Park Rugby Football ground!

We could have snatched the glider out when the weather improved but the powers that be, quite rightly, decided it should be dismantled and brought home by road. Low flying over a major city and snatching a glider was not to be encouraged even if it had a 90% chance of success!

It is difficult, in this day and age, when helicopters and aircraft can ascend and descend vertically from a space the size of a tennis court to appreciate the efforts which were made during World War II to put men into battle by dropping them by means other than individual parachute descents.

One somewhat bizarre, though nevertheless quite practical idea, was tried by the Development Unit in the form of a large aluminium box carried on the bottom of a bomber aircraft as an external load. This was called the paratechnicon. The prototype was built to fasten on to a Halifax aircraft and in its final form was to hold some 30 soldiers sitting 15 each side facing each other. On being released from the aircraft the paratechnicon would deploy six huge parachutes on which it would descend to the ground. While it descended a rubber skirt would drop somewhat akin to the skirts on hovercraft today. This skirt had a rubber floor to it with holes in to let in the air and 'windows' of thin rubber in the sides. On impact with the ground the 'windows' would blow out and the paratechnicon, in theory, was supposed to 'nest down like a sitting hen'.

The project was abandoned, due to the introduction of the helicopter, and although many successful drops were made with the paratechnicon loaded with a jeep and trailer, no drops were ever made with men inside. On one occasion twelve eggs in a strong paper bag were taped to the driver's seat in the jeep before dropping. On opening the paratechnicon after landing, every egg was broken but the system did show promise.

Murphy's Law again reared its head during the RAF Abingdon 'At Home' Day 1950. It was a lovely sunny day with a 10 knot westerly wind. Ideal for the occasion. A great spectacle had been laid on for the public with a 'fort' to be bombed and blown up; a 'downed' aviator to be rescued by our first R6 helicopter; an experienced pilot, disguised as a drunken civilian, to leave the spectator's enclosure and 'steal' a Tiger Moth which had purposely been left unattended with its engine ticking over and as a finale the paratechnicon was to be dropped containing a jeep and trailer from a Halifax Bomber.

The R6 helicopter was to be flown by Major Bernard Repton who had persuaded an RAF pilot friend to sit in the rubber dinghy on the grass as the 'downed pilot in the sea'. At the appropriate moment Bernard would fly over him, kick a rope ladder out of the doorway, whereupon the downed pilot would catch the end of it and climb up into the helicopter. Meanwhile the rubber dinghy, relieved of its passenger would be blown helter skelter across the airfield. The behaviour of the rubber dinghy normally interested the crowd far more than the downed pilot's feat of climbing up a rope ladder against the downdraught of the helicopter's blades while dangling in mid-air. Such was the state of the art of air/sea rescue by helicopter in 1950.

The paratechnicon had been dropped before many times most successfully. Because of its great size, enormous parachutes and rubber landing bags, it looked most spectacular during its descent.

Before loading all switches were checked. First of all the Master Switch was activated and found serviceable and then the bombing switch was pressed. All worked perfectly, but unspotted by the technicians, the bombing switch button had stuck down and was replaced in its holder still stuck down! The Master Switch was put back to safe not to be operated again until the run up to the target. Murphy's Law was now primed.

I was on top of the control tower giving the commentary and had just informed the crowd what a splendid spectacle they were about to see.

'The aircraft is turning in now for his final run in — just one minute to go...'

To my horror a mile away from the airfield the paratechnicon had already detached itself from the Halifax and was floating quietly down over what appeared to be the Cowley Area.

Bernard Repton was still sitting in his helicopter with engine running alongside the tower so, handing the microphone over, I dashed down and jumped in alongside him. He'd seen what had happened and we were airborne while the paratechnicon was still in sight.

While my thoughts were dominated by the inevitability of the coming Court of Enquiry, I also had enough sympathy to hope that the paratechnicon would not land on any citizen over that built up area but I knew that this was perhaps a forlorn hope.

The paratechnicon disappeared behind some trees but we were soon hovering over it. It had landed in the garden of one of two semi-detached cottages and the parachutes, all six of them, were spread over the vegetable garden and clothes line.

There was movement under the parachute silk and a woman suddenly appeared on top of the parachutes as though swimming in a surfladen sea.

Bernard landed in the field alongside and I jumped the fence into the garden fearing the worst.

Considering what she had been through the lady was far more composed than I was.

'Has anyone been hurt? Is there anyone still underneath it?'

'No', she replied in a broad Berkshire accent. 'I was just pegging out my clothes when a shadow blotted out the sun and this great thing was right over me. What did you drop it here for?'

Overjoyed that no one was hurt I stood in the gooseberry bushes explaining that the load had mysteriously detached itself from the aircraft on the run in to Abingdon aerodrome and how sorry we were to have frightened her and flattened her garden.

'Tis a pity', she said, 'but I know you wouldn't do it deliberate. I think we ought to have a cup of tea. The kettle's on the boil. Ask your friend in that there whirligig if he'd like a cup.'

Filled with relief and admiration for this worthy unflappable woman I climbed the garden fence, told Bernard the situation and called up RAF Abingdon on the helicopter radio asking for the recovery party to be sent to the cottages by Sandford Lock village. Then we retired into the cottage and partook of tea!

When the recovery party arrived we collected the parachutes, removed some fencing, took the end off the paratechnicon and drove the jeep and trailer out, into the field and on to the road. Only then did our hostess, now distributing tea to the recovery party, fully realize that she might have been killed for she thought the paratechnicon was 'just an empty box'! The crane then came in the field, and lifted the paratechnicon back on to its trailer. We put up the fence, said goodbye to our host and Bernard and I flew back in 'that there whirligig' to the airfield, both of us feeling rather humble after our brief encounter with such a noble lady.

During this era the helicopter was a comparative newcomer to the Royal Air Force. The one allotted to the unit was an American 'Hoverfly', usually known as an 'R6'. It was powered by a Franklin engine.

Curiously it took me longer to go solo on the R6 than it did to go solo on a fixed wing aircraft. This I believe is normal. It may be something to do with the fixed wing pilot's inherent fear of flying slowly.

179

But I did fly it in the end though I was never really happy flying helicopters; indeed at that time I rather dismissed the helicopter as a transitory flying machine, like the airship, which had come and gone and I felt that maybe the helicopter would be the same for surely something better would be developed.

My quarrel with the helicopter was the intense vibration. You needed both hands and feet and your teeth in order to fly it. Furthermore your life seemed to depend on one nut holding the rotor blades in position and so short a life had these blades that they had to be removed and x-rayed every fifty flying hours to see if they were developing cracks.

How and why a helicopter flies is a subject on which every expert seems to hold a different opinion. Some time later I was present at a Board of Enquiry as to why a helicopter tumbled on its side after landing normally at RAF Northolt. It was intriguing to hear the various experts' opinions as to the forces acting on a helicopter during landing and frankly the enquiry did nothing to enhance my regard for the designer/maufacturer or our own RAF aerodynamicist, for they were at loggerheads with each other when it came to explaining what really happened on touchdown!

My own education was such that I was unable to follow entirely their more abstruse explanations but it seemed that the helicopter was in the bumblebee category i.e. theoretically it can't fly but it does.

Helicopters have improved enormously since my first quarrel with them in 1949. My own theory as to how they fly may not be correct but it's how I think they fly and I did manage to clamber round the skies without breaking one so I must have got some of the theory right.

To fly the R6 you sat on the left hand side of the cockpit. Your feet controlled the rudder pedals which in turn adjusted the pitch of the little propeller at the back. This enabled you to maintain direction. This little propeller was necessary because the big rotor blades flashing round over your head really wanted to stay still and turn the fuselage round, the place where you were sitting, instead! In fact life was one long argument between the large rotor blades on top and the small propeller at the back.

Your left hand held the control column between your knees and when your mental condition had become adjusted you could regard this control, to a degree, like the control column in a fixed wing aircraft. Your left thumb and forefinger held the map.

Your right hand also had two jobs to do. It lifted and lowered a long large lever called the rotor pitch control and your right hand grasped a twistgrip throttle at the end of this lever. Having been involved with motor cycles in prewar days I was not enamoured of this twistgrip throttle. However, it must be said that despite my fear of this control jamming or the cable shearing I never experienced any trouble with it.

In flight, it was not possible to release any of the controls for more than a fraction of a second at a time as you vibrated your way across the heavens and your teeth were necessary to help turn over the map held by the thumb and forefinger of the left hand on the control column.

It was easy to understand why a helicopter went up and down vertically. Increasing the engine power with the twistgrip and bringing up the pitch control would make it leave the ground but why would it go forwards, backwards and sideways often when you didn't want it to?

Here we come into the realm of the aerodynamicists and bumblebee designers and it does not behove a general duties pilot, educated only to a prewar standard of school certificate, to delve too deeply into the these matters; but it seemed to me that in order to go forward the big rotor blades, when they got to the front, changed their pitch and became coarser as they passed down the port side and when they got to the back they feathered themselves and came back up the starboard side more or less freewheeling; so in effect it was like paddling a canoe on one side only from the middle of the canoe. The little propeller on the back helped to keep the 'canoe' straight.

To make it go sideways and backwards was easy enough from the pilot's point of view but incredible things happened in the linkage between his control column and the rotor blades. The man who designed this linkage obviously got his inspiration from studying the bell crank system in Victorian country houses which summoned servants from beyond the green baize door.

While all hands and feet were needed to make the R6 fly, the eyes also were fully occupied. At take off especially, they had to be glued to two gauges, one giving engine revolutions and the other the revolutions of the rotor blades and the relationship between the two was criticial and was achieved by the right wrist and the angle of the right elbow. Thank goodness it wasn't necessary to worry about the revolutions of the little propeller at the back. It was absolutely essential to keep these two sets of revolutions in the correct relationship to each other. At the same time you had to look out of the canopy to see what you were going to hit just as you left the ground.

Having become airborne life became easier though all hands, feet and both eyes were required. The first thing was to climb to 300 feet for between the ground and 300 feet was the death zone. Any engine failure below 300 feet meant tragedy. Above 300 feet it was a different matter for then, in theory, you had enough height to carry out an 'autorotation' in the event of an engine failure.

If the engine did fail you merely had to point the aircraft at the ground in front of you and hurl yourself to apparent destruction. This manoeuvre was actually quite safe for it made the big rotors spin round (autorotate) and so build up kinetic energy which you could use to give you lift and flatten out your glide just as you reached the ground.

Flying the R6 on instruments was by no means easy. The special instruments needed by helicopters had not yet been developed. Only the instruments used in fixed wing aircraft were available and were by no means suitable. For instance, in a fixed wing aircraft if the litle aeroplane on the artificial horizon was above the horizon you could safely assume that you were climbing up to the heavens. In the R6 you could actually be going down and backwards with your nose up! It could be confusing.

The vertical landing and take off of helicopters made them of especial interest in the clandestine role to take agents into and out of enemy territory, a role fulfilled in the Second World War by the Lysanders and Hudsons of 138 and 161 Squadrons of Tempsford.

The helicopter was obviously going to be a vast improvement on the fixed wing aircraft — if we could fly them at night.

It wasn't until I carried a simulated clandestine operation in the R6 that I discovered how very difficult it was to find a reception in peacetime. Had the Germans but realised it they could have prevented the majority of our clandestine operations in France being successful if they had abandoned the restrictions on blackout, for it was practically impossible to find the usual light patterns made by torches held by the reception committee members when there was no blackout. There were so many other lights!

The first trial was to be a 'pick up' somewhere near Kingston Bagpuize in the Vale of White Horse. At first it was a clear, star-studded January night. There was no moon. I took off from RAF Abingdon full of confidence and thought it would be an easy trip.

It was no great distance to fly to Kingston Bagpuize, but where was the reception committee? There were lights everywhere. How much easier it was to find receptions during the war in the blackout. In the end I found the reception by flying up and down the A420 following car headlights and determining my position by the pubs.

At last I found the dim torchlights of the reception and picked up the 'agent' and started vibrating my way back to

Abingdon but by now a fog bank had rolled in and I had to take to the meagre instruments. I arrived back at base thankful but very chastened. It had not been an easy trip.

Helicopters have improved since then and surprisingly they are still with us but it will be interesting to see if they are still an accepteed form of transport by the end of this century.

The Development Unit has perhaps a greater awareness of flying safety than civil aviation because military transport aircraft were expected to operate not only to their maximum limitations on take off and landing but also to experience incidents due to enemy action to prevent the delivery of the military passengers. Hence the research into backward facing seats. But there were other factors to study. One of these was the requirement to deliver airborne troops to their destination in a first class fighting condition. More often than not this was difficult to attain due to air sickness.

Innumerable drugs were tried and while some advance was made and is still being made, all drugs reduced the efficiency of the fighting soldier caused by drowsiness or induced thirst.

Some very efficient anti-sickness pills are available to the public today but almost all of them contain a warning regarding drowsiness or thirst and an exhortation not to take them if required to handle machinery; hardly the correct prescription for a soldier going into battle with complex weaponry.

While one hardly entertains 'incidents' during take offs and landings of civil aircraft, they do occur and there is no doubt that some civil passengers, having taken their pills two hours before flight as prescribed, emplane like zombies clutching their duty free molotof cocktails. Their chances of a rapid and successful evacuation of the aircraft should an incident occur, either on take off or landing, is thus reduced. But one must sympathise with the minority who would rather risk death in a very unlikely incident than suffer the horrors of air sickness.

Meanwhile the Royal Air Force and the Royal Navy are still searching for the perfect antidote.

CHAPTER 13

Suspicions

Spring was in the air. Two mad March hares cavorted near the main runway, and over by the perimeter track two partridges were gliding in for an 'engines off' landing.

It was nice to see the partridges pairing off, yet, despite the springlike scene, I was far from contented as I surveyed the airfield from my office in the control tower. It was that man de Laune again.

What was it the previous Wing Commander Flying had said to me on handing over? 'De Laune is a first class controller, quite unflappable in an emergency. He's just the boy to have with you in a tight spot and,' he added ominously, 'he's just the chap to get you into one!'

He'd been right, dead right. But de Laune, despite one or two peccadilloes, was the sort of person with whom it was difficult to get angry. He had such a charming personality it was impossible not to like him.

There was no doubt that things did get over-complicated whenever I had any dealings with de Laune and yet I couldn't blame him for my present embarrassment.

De Laune was a keen follower of the horses. At breakfast in the Mess each morning he would be absorbed in his study of the racing paper, and it was quite a while before I realised that there seemed to be a hush in the flying training pro gramme round about 3.30 p.m. in the afternoons when de

Laune was on duty in the tower. Eventually I discovered that training aircraft were asked to clear the circuit at this time while the big race was on, and Air Traffic Control was as hushed as a cathedral cloister while de Laune and his minions listened in to the big race!

And then there had been his attempts to cultivate the acquaintance of the Premier Jockey.

Our airfield was in the Vale of White Horse, some three or four miles from the Downs. On occasions when the Downs were covered with low cloud the Premier Jockey, unable to land at his own private airfield, would divert to our base. Here he would invariably partake of a cup of tea in the control tower while transport was sent over for him from his home. De Laune was not slow to bring the conversation round to horseracing but the great man was always cagey in his opinions and refused to give any tips despite de Laune's Irish charm.

Then one day when escorting the Premier Jockey to his car de Laune's charm prevailed when he asked 'You wouldn't have anything for Saturday I suppose?' The Premier Jockey laughingly replied, 'Well if you don't really mind losing half a crown you might try "Moon's Delight" in the 3.30.'

By Saturday every cent which could be raised by the personnel of Air Traffic Control had been placed on 'Moon's Delight'. She came in last. The Premier Jockey had got his message across loud and clear.

Now I had a misunderstanding due to de Laune and it was entirely my fault.

The Station Commander had recently gone on leave, leaving me in charge of the camp with a half serious, half humorous admonition 'Not to forget to have a snap check of the accounts.' I did not relish the extra responsibility. Administration was not my strong point and during a previous posting to this station I had been present when a financial scandal of considerable proportion had been uncovered. A very astute airman had brought on to the books a 'ghost' squadron of some thirty airmen and had succeeded in collecting the pay of these as yet unborn airmen. The system was really the reverse of the Naval malpractices in Nelson's day when dead sailors were deliberately kept on the books so that the paymasters could benefit.

It would be invidious of me to reveal how the 'ghost squadron' system was worked because it could be done again, and no doubt will be some day. Suffice it to say that all the 'ghost' airmen paid their dues to the RAF Benevolent Fund to avoid being interviewed by the Commanding Officer who might ask why they wouldn't contribute! While not closely involved, this previous scandal had made me nervous, especially as I could never really make head or tail of balance sheets though, curiously, I could cope with the mathematics of astro navigation.

Soon after I took over command, when coming out of breakfast one morning, I saw de Laune and the Accountant Officer in the ante-room bent over the racing paper in deep consultation.

That the Accountant Officer should be studying form with de Laune surprised me. I recalled that the Cheltenham Gold Cup was being run on this very day.

My duty was clear, I must order a snap check of the station accounts.

I waited on tenterhooks in the CO's office in Station Headquarters while the check was carried out, and my peace of mind was not helped when I enquired of the adjutant how the check was going and received the reply that they hadn't been able to open the safe because the Accountant Officer had forgotten his keys and had returned to his quarters for them.

'Ye Gods', I thought, 'he could be dashing off to Cheltenham with a suitcase of money while we wait patiently for him to return with the keys.'

I built up my morale by assuring myself that things like

this didn't happen in the Royal Air Force, and then, at last, I saw the Accountant Officer park his car and re-enter the headquarters.

And the outcome? The accounts and cash were all in order!

But one couldn't have an Accountant Officer who followed the horses.

It was a distasteful task, but I must take the matter further.

At lunchtime a day later I found myself standing next to the Accountant Officer at the bar.

'Did you do any good at Cheltenham yesterday?' I asked.

'Cheltenham, Sir? I'm afraid I don't understand. I haven't been to Cheltenham.'

'I mean the races at Cheltenham, I saw you studying the racing paper in the ante-room yesterday after breakfast with de Laune. Did you pick any winners?'

'Sir, I wasn't studying form,' he said chuckling. 'I was helping de Laune fill in his travel claim form, which was on top of the newspaper!'

And then came the night when the York was in trouble.

A civil freighter York aircraft was flying in bad weather at night from Ireland to London Airport loaded with two racehorses. First one generator failed and then somewhere near Bristol the aircraft suffered a complete electrical failure.

The pilot on sighting a beacon flashing red once every second decided to circle it. He thought it was an airfield beacon, and to draw attention to his plight he alternately increased and decreased the pitch controls of his propellers so that those on the ground would realise that he was in difficulties.

But he failed to rouse any interest. This wasn't surprising as he was, in fact, circling an atomic research station some five miles south of our airfield and the beacon signified a prohibited flying area!

Five miles to the north, however, the ululating engines were heard by one of de Laune's airmen called Thwaite, who had the good sense to switch on the airfield lighting and contact de Laune in the bar of the Officers' Mess. As de Laune arrived at the tower the York landed with the usual cacophony of crackling associated with Rolls Royce engines.

And so the aircraft and its complement of crew and racehorses were saved, and letters of congratulation fell like confetti on the station and air traffic control in particular.

But I did not feel happy about the incident. How was it that Thwaite on such a wild night should be on top of the control tower, from which his line of sight and hearing towards the atomic station to the south was interrupted by the propinquity of the hangers? I knew that Thwaite and one or two other airmen slept in the tower in preference to the overcrowded barrack blocks, but it seemed odd that he should be up on the tower in such inclement weather.

And then how was it that de Laune had arrived at the tower so speedily, for on talking to the pilot he had landed within about three minutes of seeing the airfield lights switched on?

But I must dispel these suspicions. I had already made a fool of myself once over the Cheltenham Cup incident. Sufficient to sit back and bask in the eulogies falling on the station, and my department in particular.

I was not surprised that Thwaite was the architect of this glory. A solid North Country National Serviceman, he had made a name for himself in the tower for his reliability and initiative.

In de Laune's well run, though unorthodox, organisation Thwaite could turn his hand to anything from handling taxiing aircraft over the radio to making tea. Thwaite and de Laune were a formidable pair to have in any organisation.

Then tragedy struck.

I arrived at my flying wing headquarters in the tower one morning to find de Laune waiting. He looked embarrassed.

'I'm afraid I have a charge pending Sir. It's Thwaite. He pranged the "Follow Me" vehicle last night.'

At this time all strange aircraft were met as they turned off the runway by a vehicle with a 'Follow Me' or 'Suivez moi' board on the back, which could be illuminated at night so that they could be directed to their parking place.

It was bad luck that Thwaite, the saviour of the York and the most willing and reliable airman in the tower should prang the pick-up! But justice must be done. A charge had to be made.

In due course the short stocky Thwaite was wheeled in hatless between two of the biggest service policemen on the station.

The proceedings continued. Thwaite made his statement. He had been sent out by Flight Lieutenant de Laune in the 'Follow Me' pick-up to lead in a Dakota en route to the Middle East, which was to collect engine spares in the movements area without stopping engines.

As Thwaite sped along the perimeter track at the southern end of the airfield he could see the Dakota's red port wing-tip light, and then he suddenly saw the green starboard light, and at the same time the Dakota pilot had switched on his wing landing light.

Thwaite then graphically described how, blinded by the landing light, he swung the pick-up off the perimeter track and put his foot on the accelerator to get clear and ended up by driving into one of the concrete posts which were being erected for the new airfield perimeter fencing.

It was hard luck. He had avoided the unforgiveable sin of colliding with an aircraft but he had pleaded guilty.

And so the saviour of the York was, in the circumstances, awarded the minimum sentence — a reprimand, and after the crashing of feet and the bawling and shouting of withdrawal had subsided I mused on the injustices of this world. What bad luck that a splendid chap like Thwaite should get caught out like that!

The months passed and, as is the way in the Royal Air Force, personalities were posted to other stations including de Laune who went to Germany.

Then came a day when I found Thwaite's documents on my desk all ready for signing on his discharge, having now completed his national service. Thwaite was marched in to say goodbye; this time with his hat on.

He seemed hesitant and embarrassed. To put him at his ease I muttered the usual platitudes and referred to his initiative on landing the York with the racehorses.

I was about to shake hands with him when he said, 'Sir, may I have a word with you in private?'

I nodded to the adjutant and he withdrew.

'Before I go, Sir,' said Thwaite, 'I feel I must tell you the truth about that accident I had with the pick-up that night. You see I didn't hit a concrete post. I shot the top of the radiator and bonnet with a 12-bore.'

'Really,' I said, 'tell me more.'

'Flight Lieutenant de Laune and I were shooting on the airfield in the headlights of the pick-up. One of us drove and the other stood up in the back to shoot over the cab. It was the Flight Lieutenant's turn to drive and my turn to shoot and suddenly this hare we had been chasing stopped and I shot the radiator by mistake. We realised that we were in a difficult situation and Flight Lieutenant de Laune hit on the idea of belting the radiator with one of the concrete posts.

'So the Dakota had nothing to do with it?' I queried.

'Not really, Sir. It was after the Dak had left for Malta that we went out to douse the Money flares and took the 12-bore with us.'

'And am I right in thinking that Flight Lieutenant de Laune thought up the story about you being dazzled by the Dakota's landing light?'

'Yes,' replied Thwaite.

The previous suspicions made me ask, 'Tell me, Thwaite, would I be right in thinking that on the night you saved the York you were not on top of the tower? You and de Laune were out shooting on the airfield?'

'Yes, Sir.' 'You're quite right, Sir. You see we couldn't say what we were doing at the time.' 'But,' he added, 'it was lucky that we were out with the gun or we should never have heard the aircraft.'

So, at last the truth was out. I felt relieved and warmed to Thwaite. He had no need to tell me but obviously he had a conscience.

'I'm glad to know the truth, Thwaite. I always felt that there was something odd about the York story. You know that you are still subject to the Air Force Act until your leave expires, but I think you deserve all the praise you've had. The cost of a Hillman radiator and bonnet is nothing compared with a York aircraft saved.'

Some years later I attended a guest night at which a famous American General replied to the toast of the guests. He spoke of the spirit of the Royal Air Force, its unusual form of humour especially in the face of adversity and the remarkable way in which RAF personnel could always devise something to amuse and occupy themselves in uncivilised places; and above all, the extraordinary way in which, in a military organisation, they were able to preserve their own individuality.

The glittering silverware, the medals, the shiny buttons and the white shirt-fronts faded in the soft light of the guttering candles. In the wraiths of the cigar smoke I visualised two men bashing the top of a Hillman radiator with a concrete post.

'Ability to occupy themseves and preserve their individuality.'

Glossary

AC_2	Aircraftsman 2nd Class
ACH	Aircrafthand
AI	Air Interception
ASV	Anti Surface Vessel
BLEU	Blind Landing Experimental Unit
Clag	RAF expression denoting unbroken cloud which is of some depth and solid from bottom to top
Erk	A term of endearment denoting the lowest ranks of the RAF
ETA	Estimated Time of Arrival
GCA	Ground Controlled Approach. Sophisticated equipment on the ground enabled a controller to land any type of aircraft provided the aircraft carried a transmitter/receiver
GCI	Ground Controlled Interception
Gee	A medium range navigational aid of great accuracy so long as the receiving aircraft was within 'optical' range of the transmitter. One transmitter during the war was on the top of Snowdon
H_2S	An airborne 10 cm navigational and bombing aid. On the cathode ray tube it gave startling pictures of land features, towns, rivers, coastlines etc.

ILS	Instrument Landing System formerly known as the American Signals Corps System 51 (SCS 51)
ITF	Inter Tropical Front. A band of extremely bad weather which moves above and below the equator according to the time of year. As its cumulo-nimbus cloud towers up to 30,000 feet propeller driven aircraft still have to face up to flying through it on North/South routes
Ko	Siamese for island
Mandrel	Jammer against 'Freya' radars
Monica	Radar device fitted to bombers to warn of approaching night fighters. Not popular as it increased the 'Funk Factor'. Eventually abandoned as we discovered that German night fighters were homing on to 'Monica'
Money Flare	A 1914/18 wartime invention for marking an airfield for landing at night. It consisted of what looked like an outsize engineers' oil can which held some 2 gallons of paraffin. A wick protruded from the $1\frac{1}{2}$ diameter spout and the flame produced was not only superior to electric lights in foggy conditions but very distinctive and helped identify the position of an airfield when laid as a 'flarepath'
Murphy's Law	If a piece of equipment is designed so that it can be taken apart and reassembled incorrectly someone some day will do just that. Aircraft designers are very much aware of Murphy's Law and try to eliminate its presence in their designs. They are not always successful
NO	Naval Officer
Oboe	An extremely accurate high altitude bombing device
Pulo or Puloh	The Malay word for island or the figure nought

Rebecca/
Eureka   A small Eureka beacon on the ground could be triggered off by Rebecca equipment carried in an aircraft. This enabled the aircraft to home on to the Eureka and also measure his distance from it

Serrate   Fitted to Mosquitoes. It was a radar set which could home on to German airborne radar.

Postscript

What happened to some of the characters in this story is related in order of their appearance:

Leading Aircraftsman Templeton
> The signaller and 'sole navigational aid' on the flight to Singapore. Last seen fighting off three Japanese Zeros near Port Swetenham, Malaya, in December 1941.

Group Captain Oliver Bryson MC, DFC, and bar, AM
> OC RAF Tengah renowned for the Tiger Skin Incident. Retired 1943 and died during the 1960s.

Flying Officer Harley Boxall
> (later Group Captain). Flew bombing missions against the Japanese from Singapore, Sumatra and Java. 62 Squadron was decimated and he escaped to Australia. Posted to India and invalided out of the RAF in 1946. Has since lived in Zimbabwe where he is a senior executive in the motor industry.

'Paddy' Calvert
> Navigator to 'Pongo' Scarf on his last flight. Survived the war. Now living in Auckland, New Zealand. A

keen free fall parachutist still jumping in his sixties.

Ken Hutchins

My sailing companion to Pulo Pisang and one of the Blenheim pilots who flew out to Singapore. Got away from Singapore and finally ended up in Kenya. Returned to the UK and converted on to Dakotas. On 'D' day set off in first wave of airborne troops. Nothing was heard of him or his crew again.

J W S Pringle

The zoologist who read a book about radio on his way for interview for recruitment as a radar scientist. After five very productive years at TRE returned to his first love at Oxford. Subsequently MBE, FRS, Professor of Zoology, Fellow of Merton College.

A P Rowe

Superintendent of TRE. Subsequently wrote a book the title of which was indicative of his respect for other people's feelings. He called it 'One Story of Radar' knowing that others would write on the subject and probably claim 'first in the field'.

Douglas Fisher

The photographer impervious to hypothermia and companion on many Walrus flights. Postwar formed Douglas Fisher Audio Visual Ltd, Mistley, making Natural History films for TV and Research films for the Wellcome Trust.

Gabe Robb Bryce OBE

'Jock' to the RAF. As a navigator at TRE he had plenty of opportunity to act as co-pilot on occasions and take over pilot duties for straight and level flying. He showed such great aptitude that one aircraft captain, after letting him practise 'cloud landings' in an Anson aircraft, allowed him to carry out his first real landing in the aircraft which was not equipped with dual controls. It says much for his judgement in that Jock duly qualified as a pilot and for 14 years was Chief Test Pilot for Vickers Armstrongs.

Wrens Jackson, Sharp and Palmer

Unsuccessful attempts were made to contact these unsung heroines via *Navy News* in 1985. They are probably grey-haired grandmothers today with fading memories of cold, sick-making trips in wallowing Walruses, Swordfishes and Sea Otters yet what a contribution they made to winning the Battle of the Atlantic!

Dr A M Uttley

Inventor of the Submarine Bombing Trainer. Became Supertintendent Autonomics Division, National Physics Laboratory and later Research Professor of Experimental Psychology, University of Sussex. Died in September 1985.

Lieutenant M H Jupp DSC, RN

Captain of submarine H 33. Subsequently Captain of submarine *HMS Syrtis* which was lost off Bodo, Norway, in March 1944.

Lieutenant T D Wood DSC, RNVR

First Lieutenant of H 33 who left the vessel at Moville, Donegal, to fly to London by Walrus, Liberator and Dakota. After the war spent 25 years in New Guinea partly as a merchant and partly at sea. Eventually bought his own ship and was one of the last 'blackbirders'. Retired to Brisbane, Australia in 1974 where he ran a 25-knot, 200 passenger catamaran to Moreton Island. At the age of 70 there is a photograph showing him holding two baby girls both three months old. One is his great grandchild and the other his own daughter; living proof that submarining has no effect on fertility.

Lieutenant G Gellie DSC, Royal Australian Navy

Took over as First Lieutenant on H 33 on departure of Lt Wood from Moville. Subsequently served in *HMAS Penguin*. On demobilisation joined De Beers Industrial Diamonds. Retired in 1985. Now lives in Melbourne.

Lieutenant Commander A E Milward, RNVR

Officer Commanding Naval Section of Telecommunications Flying Unit whose introduction of intelligent girls, members of the Womens Royal Naval Service, both into the laboratories and flight testing of airborne radar devices, saved many 'man' hours. Subsequently knighted and became Chairman of British European Airways.

Colonel Francis L Moseley, US Army Air Force

Whose 'black box' demonstrations 'sold' Automatic Landings to the British. In the field of aeronautical electronics he held over 50 patents including the basic patent for Automatic Direction Finding (ADF). Today his system is still the basic principle on which Automatic Landings are made. He continued all his life to invent and develop servo-actuated instruments and devices. A Director of the Hewlett Packard Company. A quiet man with a tremendous sense of humour he died 25th May 1984 in Pasadena, California.

Frank B Brady

The US scientist from Wright Field assistant to

Colonel Moseley. After World War II when piloting a C 47 (Dakota) flew into a flock of ducks which shattered his windscreen. He managed to land the aircraft safely but emerged from hospital having lost one eye.

At a party to celebrate his discharge from hospital he refuelled a guest's glass from a jug by pouring the cocktail down her dress.

This started him on a series of studies and experiments to achieve stereoscopic effect when using only one eye. These studies culminated in a book entitled 'A Singular View' now accepted by opthalmologists on both sides of the Atlantic as the most suitable literature for the newly one-eyed trying to cope with his new condition.

Brady subsequently continued with work in connection with the blind landing of helicopters and aircraft. Currently he is Editor of the United States *Journal of Navigation*.

Group Captain J A McDonald CBE, AFC
The Officer Commanding RAF Defford who lost his rudder while flying a Spitfire. Subsequently civilian Commandant of Prestwick International Airport then Deputy Commandant of London Airport. Died 17th April 1983, aged 85.

Flying Officer L C Barber
Known as 'Figaro'. Companion on many of the early automatic landings and compulsive inventor of things electronic. After demobilisation, despite lucrative offers of employment in the United States, he formed his own company at Worthing where he designed and manufactured the 'Pinta' automatic pilot for trawlers, yachts and small craft.

Colwyn Stone

One of the 'Widecombe Fair' quartet at the Blind Landing Experimental Unit. An 'ace' trouble-shooter and diagnostician in the field of avionics. After BLEU employed by Smiths Instruments, Cheltenham, then GEC, Maidstone, researching in both avionics and instrumentation for the North Sea Oil Industry. On the 9th December 1979 he died at the wheel of his stationary car in Chatham.

Index

205

INDEX